HOUSE RICH CASH POOR NO MORE!

HOW TO USE THE EQUITY IN YOUR HOME TO ACHIEVE FINANCIAL FREEDOM

DAVID RHODD

ISBNs

Ebook: 978-1-989059-03-6

Paperback: 978-1-989059-02-9

Hardcover: 978-1-989059-05-0

Audiobook: 978-1-989059-04-3

PRAISE FOR DAVID RHODD

"This excellent book teaches you a practical, proven method to get out of debt, build a financial reserve, buy a home (or homes) and achieve financial freedom for life!"

— BRIAN TRACY, AUTHOR OF MORE THAN 70 BOOKS, INCLUDING
THE POWER OF SELF CONFIDENCE

"David understands what the wealthy have understood for years – that one does not get rich off a paycheque! If you are looking to emulate the wealthy and are searching for an opportunity to build wealth leveraging what you quite likely already have available to you – I urge you to read on.'

— ROBINSON SMITH, PUBLISHER OF IS YOUR MORTGAGE TAX
DEDUCTIBLE? THE SMITH MANOEUVRE AND PRESIDENT OF
SMITH CONSULTING GROUP

DEDICATION

To my three children, Jada, Preston and Eliott. You are all brilliant and unique in your own way. This book is evidence that you already have within yourself anything that you need to achieve greatness in life. You have inspired me to stand up and be different, to fight through failure, self-confidence set-backs and fear to get to this point. It was all worth it because it was for you.

CONTENTS

ACKNOWLEDGMENTS

It's amazing the joy that I get out of life by having the right knowledge and support system, the fearless nature to take action, and in being open to failure. There were many things I thought I would become in life, but being an author was not one of them. Numerous people poured time and energy into my life, including my high school teachers, church family, Magna work colleagues, business professionals in my industry, and my friends. I've enjoyed the longevity and commitment of our relationships over the years. I've taken all the gems from your advice and experiences and kept them in my back pocket to be used during this journey that we call life.

To my mentors, whom you will read about in the coming pages, I am so grateful that years ago you each had the insight and foresight to write a book about your experiences. Each of you has produced a book that has helped, and continues to help, boost the lives of millions of readers, including my own, for the better. You inspired me to write about my experience so that I can hope to provide similar help to others.

When I started on this book-writing journey, I had no idea of the magnitude of effort and support that this project would require. I extend special thanks to my editor, Boni Wagner-Stafford, who took all my technical mumbo jumbo and turned it into the readable masterpiece that you have in your hands today. Also special thanks to my advance copy readers who took the time to review the book with a fresh set of eyes and provide valuable feedback.

Most importantly I want to thank my wife, Leah, for her unwavering support. Through this journey, she has worn every hat possible and made an imprint in all areas of my life. Thanks for always being there for me and supporting me with all my decisions. Thanks for never wavering during our hardest times. Thanks for being my best friend, for always dreaming with me as we mapped out the future together.

Last but not least my foundation. I owe a great debt of gratitude to my parents. You made a sacrifice to start a new life miles away from what you knew in order to provide a better life for me and my siblings. You saw something within me as a child, and prepared and shaped me to be who I was destined to become. To my siblings and Auntie, thank you for showing me – the youngest – the wisdom from the paths you took before me. I've learned so much from each of you that helped me change the trajectory of my life's path.

And to you, my reader. Thank you for your time, which is something that can never be given back. You made the choice to commit a portion of your time to read this book in hopes that it may add some clarity on your journey to build wealth. I do hope you discovered some golden nuggets of inspiration.

* * *

INTRODUCTION

I grew up in middle-class Toronto, Canada. My parents were hard-working nine-to-fivers. We didn't live a lavish lifestyle by any means, but we had what we needed: food on the table, clothes to wear, and a roof over our heads.

I don't remember exactly, but it was somewhere around the end of high school or the start of college that I read Robert Kiyosaki's *Rich Dad Poor Dad*. I was too young to understand the value of having a mentor at that time, but in looking back, *Rich Dad Poor Dad*, even though it was a book, was the first to fill that role. It 'flicked the switch' for me, showing me there was a different way to do things in life, a different way to achieve things, and that it was possible to achieve different results.

I saw my parents working so hard, being so diligent and clearly very committed to providing the necessities for us kids. *Rich Dad Poor Dad* was my first inkling that maybe I could work hard in another way, achieve more than the middle class is expected to achieve, if I thought about money in a different way.

Being a teenager about to go to college, I didn't act on Kiyosaki's lessons right away. I became a mechanical technologist, got a job after graduating and found myself with a very good job at the auto parts magnate Magna International. I made good money, I travelled a lot for work, seeing new places and cultures, and it was not lost on me that I was very fortunate indeed.

But it wasn't quite what I wanted. *Rich Dad Poor Dad* was still in the back of my mind. I took a few more courses and seminars, read several more books, and step by step I started to put the concepts promoted by Kiyosaki into practice.

- It's not how much money you make, it's how much money you keep.
- The poor and the middle class work for money; the wealthy put their money to work for them.
- It's not the smart that get ahead, but the bold.
- Build your assets first, and stop focusing on your hourly wage.
- Those who avoid failure also avoid success.
- The most powerful asset is your mind: use it well and you can create enormous wealth.

Rich Dad Poor Dad became a bible of sorts. Even though I'd never met Kiyosaki, I felt as though he was speaking directly to me, imparting wisdom and providing a glimpse into a world of possibilities I had not seen before. I was able to take action and see results based on his teachings.

However, I was still getting stuck in the penny-wise, pound-foolish mindset. For the longest time, I continued to do my own taxes. My mindset was that I'd spend $20 on the software and spend a few hours, rather than spend $200 for an accountant. I mean, $200! It seemed like so much to me.

Year after year I repeated the process, and not once did I get a refund. The first time I bit the bullet and tried the accountant route, I got a refund that more than covered the $200 fee. It was another 'flick the switch' moment: I realized that the accountant is the master at what he does, and it was shortsighted of me not to invest in professional accounting services to help me make the most of my time and money.

Later in the book, I'll show you some simple steps to help you improve your financial situation. In my business now, I focus on helping home buyers and home owners who hate dealing with mortgages and financial issues. My clients want to work with an expert who understands their needs, who can navigate mortgage issues, and who can help them use the equity in their homes to build wealth for them and their children. I help build road maps so my clients are always clear how their financial products, particularly related to their home, are working to help them achieve their goals.

I have assisted many Canadians in arranging mortgages that are optimized to allow them to build wealth and pay those mortgages off faster, saving them thousands of dollars in interest. Using my diverse knowledge of alternative investments including foreign exchange, commodities, real estate and mortgage investing, I have assisted and coached many to realize above average returns on their investment portfolios and liquid cash, thus allowing them to enjoy more fulfilling lives.

House Rich Cash Poor? No More! is about helping you increase your financial capacity, build a portfolio of secure investments, and boost your overall financial well-being. I will show you how to take a few simple steps that will let you live a better life. You can be free from money worries, free from credit problems, and free of the barriers preventing you from achieving your dreams.

If you already know your life purpose, you already have a vision of the life you want to live and are ready to take steps to achieve it. With this book, I will reveal a clear roadmap to help you create a better financial future.

Why Am I Here?

This is one of the questions asked most often whenever someone gives a thought to his or her existence. Since the dawn of time, it's probably been asked by almost every human who reached puberty. And yet, only a few really know the answer. Each of us has a different and unique purpose that makes our lives and the lives of others around us more fulfilling. If you aren't sure of your purpose and don't know what you really want, then that's where you'll want to start.

I don't believe in saving and investing money, planning cash flow, and buying investment properties just because it sounds good or because it might impress your friends. I believe in it because of how it can change your life.

I believe in the power of reaching a point where you aren't worried about money, but where you have complete control over your money and complete control over your life. This kind of control that comes from walking in the purpose of your life, which allows you to design the details of what you want to do, who and where you want to be, how you want to live, and what your legacy will be long after you're gone.

As you read this book, I want you to keep the idea of your purpose – finding it, articulating it, owning it – front and centre. If you're not sure how to do this, there are programs, seminars, courses, and books to learn from. (I've included a list of suggested readings at the end of this book.)

Financial Life Stages

Everybody's purpose is different, and it is affected by the financial stage they're in. My clients fit into one or more of these four financial life stages.

1. The Renter
2. The Ready to Buy
3. The Home Owner
4. The Investor.

You should recognize yourself in one of these categories.

1. The Renter

When I work with the Renter, I help him/her work toward home ownership. This includes coaching him/her on repairing credit, as may be necessary, and saving up a down payment.

The Renter is renting an apartment, a condo, or a house. The Renter works a full-time job, probably nine to five, and is likely carrying some debt. The idea of owning a home is appealing, and the Renter is probably either daydreaming about it or starting to take concrete steps toward saving up for a down payment. Although at times it can be difficult to save for that down payment because of bills, debts and other lifestyle expenses, I encourage the Renter to put away as much money as possible on a regular basis. For that client, the ideal goal is to own a home. An individual in this category sets goals to make and keep enough money to get into a house.

Sometimes it is necessary to work a second job.

When I was in the Renter stage, I remember there was not much money left at the end of the month. I started a business for my second job. I had a passion – more than anything, I wanted to help others – and I wanted something that would allow me to plan my tax affairs more efficiently. I knew my business had the potential to grow into something big, but at that time I had no idea what it would be like today.

All I knew was that I had a dream, an idea, and I executed.

And here you are, reading my book :-).

There are a few challenges for the Renter in making the step into home ownership.

1. **Repairing credit and reducing debt.** Getting and keeping an excellent credit rating is an important step for the renter wanting to buy a home. I discuss credit scores and credit ratings in chapter three. Focus on your credit, and reduce your debt as much as possible. Plan your cash flow so you can actually see that you're paying down your debts one at a time. Remember to pay them on time to increase your overall credit score.
2. **Saving enough for a down payment.** If you must work a second job for a short period of time, do it. Once you've paid off your debts, focus on putting away as much money away as you can. With your credit rating in better shape, your debts under control, and some savings accumulating, you're on the right track. You need to get into a home of your own, pay a mortgage, and feel the financial responsibility of managing every aspect of where you live, including minor and major maintenance, repairs, upgrades, utility bills, taxes, etcetera.

2. The Ready to Buy

The person who is Ready to Buy has repaired his/her credit and saved up enough for a down payment. Twenty-five per cent of the purchase price is an excellent target, but difficult to reach for some people in some areas, especially places like Vancouver and Toronto, where in December 2016 the average single-detached house price was nearly $1.5 million and just under $1 million respectively. Indeed, it has become more acceptable and often necessary to purchase a home with less than 25 per cent, sometimes 10 per cent and even 5 per cent down. There are government programs to assist first-time buyers. Check with your municipal, provincial, and national governments to see what's available in your area.

This journey to becoming a first-time home owner creates a flow of emotions: great excitement along with understandable fear and anxiety. But it is completely worth it in the end. When you begin to experience these emotions, you will know that you are on the right track. You know you are getting something that you can call your own. You have the money set aside, you have been diligent, but you might not be sure what to expect on the other side of the fence. Will the grass truly be greener?

You might wonder, "When I get in, will I be able to afford it all?" "What happens if I lose my job?" Or, "How will I manage to pay my mortgage?"

These are all legitimate, valid questions that many new home buyers ask themselves. Understand that this is normal, and nearly every new home owner before you has faced the same fears.

My suggestion is to read, research, and talk to others who have recently purchased a home and ask about their experiences. The more information you gather, the better you'll feel.

When I was in the stage of the Ready to Buy, my fears seemed over-whelming, as they should when venturing into the unknown. To calm my fears, I said a simple prayer and found a sort of peace in taking that next step into home ownership. I have never looked back. Purchasing a home is a big step, but the benefits far outweigh the fear. This step will open you up to a world of possibilities.

3. The Home Owner

Many people get to this stage and never leave. They have no concept that they could be doing more with their money, and if they do, they don't know how. Most people own their homes, but continue being stuck in their nine-to-five jobs. They may try to make extra mortgage payments at the end of the term, but overall they're still just making ends meet. This is similar to the Renter, only now they're responsible for replacing the roof.

That's why we're here and why you're reading this book. The main goal at this stage is to pay down the mortgage as fast as possible. When you own your home, it's important to continue making money management a priority. Control and monitor your expenses, maxi-mize your income.

My clients in the Home Owner stage learn the best way to pay down their mortgages. I help them create a power team – with an accoun-tant, a lawyer, and me – all working to build their wealth. I help them learn about becoming an investor, and the liberating power of investing to build financial independence for themselves and their family.

4. The Investor

The Investor is ready to use and leverage the equity within his/her home to purchase other properties and/or other investments. These investments create cash flow every month.

The Investor can rent out or sell investment properties, and use the profits either to purchase more properties or to create their desired lifestyle while building their empire. Buy, leverage, sell, repeat.

My Client Strategy

I work with my clients, regardless which category they are in, to create a strategy specific to their financial stage as well as their unique circumstances. This strategy is designed to help them move through to the next category, and the next, until they achieve the level of financial independence they desire.

In *House Rich Cash Poor No More!*, you'll find out exactly what I tell my clients. You'll hear the real-life stories of some of my clients, whose names and circumstances I have changed to protect their identities. You'll find out why your credit score matters and how to take charge of it. You'll learn the simple steps to take to steadily reduce consumer debt, pay down loans, and reduce the balance on your mortgage.

We'll talk about the models used by the big banks to stay profitable year after year, and which approaches to adopt so you can become profitable, too. We'll discuss the reasons home ownership is a critical step on your journey to financial success. I'll show you how to generate passive income – that's money coming in that you don't have to lift a finger to attract – by leveraging the equity in your home to invest.

And we'll talk about the importance of having a coach, or a mentor, to guide you on your journey: someone who knows the ropes, who has been there before, and who can save you the heartache and cash-killers of missteps borne out of ignorance.

I'm glad you're reading this book. It can be one of your first coaches, and you don't even have to leave the house. My only interest in writing this book is to help you become financially free. That's not a decision for you to take lightly, because it will change your future. You can be the creator of your own destiny, master of your own empire, protector of your own interests. The difference between failure and success is simply never giving up on the goal, and taking action to make it happen.

Reader alert This book is meant to be interactive in nature and you'll find links and references for more information. The most important one is for what I call your backstage access. I've created summary videos of each chapter. After you've finished a chapter, go to davidrhodd.com/backstagepass and select the relevant chapter. It is FREE and will give you additional insights as you go through the book. No cheating, though! Read a chapter, then watch the video. Read another chapter, then watch the corresponding video. See you backstage.

* * *

1

MINDSET MAKES MILLIONAIRES

Have you ever wondered what makes successful people tick? What it is that makes wealthy people wealthy? What is so different about them? Maybe they came into money by fluke, or by inheritance, or maybe they had a whiz-bang accountant or investor that looked after their finances. It could be any or all of the above. But these are not the things that set the wealthy apart.

Wealthy people all have one thing in common, aside from the obvious that they are wealthy. It's just one thing. And it's not exclusive to their club. Anyone can flick the switch to get it and have it. And anyone can create it. Even you. Regardless of whether you're dead broke, bankrupt, about to be bankrupt, or just getting by, you can have it too. It's just one thing, but it is the thing. You must have it if you wish to change your financial future.

It's your mindset.

Adversity

The wealthy and the successful do not wallow in despair when they make mistakes or when times are tough. They gather what they've learned from the experience and they move on.

Adversity plays an important role in life: it teaches, it builds, it reveals.

Many quit altogether when they encounter failure, or a setback. Others simply drop their head for a moment before looking back up and moving forward with a fight.

Now, which of those attitudes and responses do you think has a higher probability of becoming successful?

Obviously, the person who fights and moves forward.

Indeed, it is how you recover and move forward that determines your success.

Adversity comes in many forms: a stolen bicycle, a flat tire on an icy highway, a job or career setback, or even something life threatening. It can be the nasty fallout from a marriage breakdown. A client I'll call Ted went through a nasty breakup and his former partner was really out to get him. It was so bad that for a while Ted was afraid to put his face on his business cards, and as a realtor that's not good news. Realtors always have their pictures on their business cards.

Ted told me one time that he was extremely upset because his ex-wife had been telling false tales about him to people in their circle and trying to poison them against him. It was a very difficult time for Ted and he was distraught. For a time. But soon Ted realized that his ex-wife was just that: ex. She wasn't in his life any longer. Then I watched as Ted chose to focus on the blessings in his life and not on the negativity being spun by his vengeful ex. Ted transformed the energy and used it for good; he ensured his life demonstrated the opposite of what his bitter former wife wanted others to see. Ted stands strengthened today.

Many people absorb all the negativity around them. They let it cripple them, sometimes without even knowing how strongly the ill will of others has affected their behaviours and thoughts. I implore and encourage you not to join their ranks. Avoid any potential evil which has the power to conquer your belief system. Use your support system to keep you strong and hold you up during the challenging times. Do not be afraid of the difficult days. They will come, and they bring lessons. Learn to be okay with that. Bad days and setbacks and enduring adversity build character.

The key takeaway is this: you are the creator of your life. Don't listen to anyone who delivers negativity into your life. Watch the words and actions of those around you. Set boundaries and then honour those boundaries by refusing to let others cross. Doing so will make it clear, to you and to them, that they cannot dictate the terms of your life. What and who others expect you to be needs to be pushed to the bottom of your concern list.

Remarkably Unremarkable

Brian Tracy, author of *Change Your Thinking, Change Your Life,* sums up his study of wealthy people by saying most of them are "remarkably unremarkable". Wealthy people do not have to be brilliant or talented, intellectual or clever. They are often honest, hardworking individuals who do not quit when things get tough. They have a life purpose. They go after what they want. They keep the big picture in mind while taking care of the small stuff. They have a mindset that naturally creates the open door for wealth to walk in.

It's the mindset of, "I can," "I am worthy," and "I deserve this."

And you must think positively about money. Just thinking negative thoughts about money can get in the way of you achieving wealth and happiness.

When you learn to think positively about money, doors of opportunity will simply begin opening before you.

There is power in that. Know that your mindset is what changes everything. Your mindset is what determines being successful, or being a failure.

It doesn't matter where you are, what you have, what mistakes you've made, what you know, what you don't know, who you have as a mentor or coach, or if you have one at all. It doesn't matter. It is a level playing field. Until you start talking about mindset.

Belief

You need to believe in yourself and believe that you can do this. You need to be confident that even if you don't have the knowledge right now of how to become wealthy, you can find it, learn it, and create it. And you need to understand that building wealth takes time. It is not an overnight procedure. It is a process. Now is the time to get a mentor, a coach, and leverage that person's experiences.

How do you believe in yourself and be confident? The first step is to flick that switch – the one in your mind. It's the first and biggest thing that stands between where you are today and reaching that goal of fulfilling your purpose while you acquire wealth and success.

Brian Tracy has published more than 70 books that outline details of the steps to take to become successful, wealthy, more effective at managing your time, even how to write a book. The common theme throughout all his materials is mindset. Tracy breaks down the shift in thinking into these five categories.

1. Design, Not Accident

Develop a purposeful mindset about building wealth and achieving financial freedom. No more blue-sky wouldn't-it-be-nice-when daydreaming. No more leaning on lottery tickets as your ticket to heaven. You must plan, design, and decide what your financial future is going to be.

2. Prosperity, Not Survival

Most people are stuck in a survival mindset. Paycheque to paycheque living, with an 'I can't afford it' mentality. The wealthy view the world differently and they did so even before they amassed their wealth. The wealthy have a mindset that is biased towards prosperity. So, for you, the task is to think about what you plan to acquire in your life and stop focusing on how little you have today.

3. Opportunity, Not Security

"Can a man change his stars?"

"Yes, William. If he believes enough, a man can do anything!"

I love this dialogue exchange from the movie *A Knight's Tale*. The late Heath Ledger's character, William, was born to a peasant father and he had to hit the road at a young age to fend for himself. He became squire to a knight, Sir Ector, learning how to be a knight in the process. Sir Ector died before he could compete in an upcoming jousting tournament, so Will decided to impersonate Sir Ector. He wore Sir Ector's armour, pretended to be him, and competed in the tournament. And won! He made friends with other noblemen, entered and won other tournaments, even won the heart of the girl. All because he believed he could 'change his stars'.

You are going to have to leave your comfort zone to change your stars. Financial freedom won't come to you if you insist on playing it safe.

4. Saving, Not Spending

We're in a spending society, there's no question. But if you plan to build wealth, you will need to shift your mindset from one of spending to one of saving. It will be a habit you will want to cultivate as well. Experts agree that what it takes to achieve financial independence is the ability to save between 20 and 30 per cent of your income. But the saving isn't what you need to focus on just yet. Focus on the mindset of a saver. Mindset comes first.

5. Doing, Not Hoping

Thinking from the warm comfort of your living room, not doing anything about your great new mindset, isn't going to get you anywhere. You need to develop a mindset of action. Just. Start.

Start putting money away, trimming your debt, taking action that will lead you to the financial freedom you have decided you want to achieve. In the end, it all comes down to your mindset and to taking action. This two-part transformation of changing your mindset and taking immediate action opens new doors. Taking just one step is not enough. Do not fail yourself by changing your mindset but forgetting to implement.

6. Forward, Not Fear

I'm adding my own number six here. The reason you might get stuck and feel unable to take action is fear. There are so many people who doubt themselves, who take courses and attend seminars, and who network and read. However, they freeze up with fear and fail to implement their new findings. They may get energized and motivated while they're reading, but then as soon as the book is closed, the fear replaces the energy and motivation and the book gets put back on the bookshelf.

When this happens, you've let fear take over, making you think you've forgotten all that you've learned, that you've forgotten about all the strategies. This is fear at work. What are you afraid of? Figure it out. Ask yourself what is the worst thing that could possibly happen. Then get back to the basics of the mindset of millionaires.

Repeat after me: "I can. I am worth it. I deserve this." Once you've tackled the fear, you will be ready to master the mindset that will allow you to use your home equity to invest, and to take all the steps needed to bring success.

So, changing your mindset, having purpose, and taking action are the three key ingredients for success. With these three components engaged, everything else will fall into place. Don't wait until you can see the end to take the first step.

And keep your money plans to yourself. Wealthy people do not talk about their money.

Be empowered to look fear in the face and conquer. Go forward and do not worry any longer about failing. If your enemies want to knock you down, let them try. You will be in a place where they can't reach you.

Changing your thinking removes the barriers and restrictions that we all set without realizing it. Get rid of self-doubt, self-loathing, any thoughts that you are unworthy. Once those boundaries are removed, you will see an immediate difference in your life. You are good enough, you are worth it, you deserve it, and you can do it.

Make your life worth it. Live with purpose. Do something different. Shake things up.

* * *

2

FIND YOUR PURPOSE WITHIN

How do you decide to do something different? How do you shake things up? How do you discover – and then fulfill – your higher life purpose? How do you do your great work, or start and run a successful business, based on your inner gifts?

How many of your decisions are affected by the lack of money? How much of what's in your heart is affected by lack of money? If you are like I was before I set out on this path, the answer is, "A lot." You too can change your financial stars. But the first step is to get your purpose crystal clear.

Your purpose will answer the question, 'Why am I here?' This book is testament to my answer to that question. One reason I have been able to write this book is because I do understand my purpose and the reason I am here, on this earth, in this country, this city, this home, and living this life.

Why are you here? What makes you tick? What would you love to do? What are you good at? How can you help others? How can you give back to your community, to society? I challenge you to look well beyond the simplistic answer 'I want to be rich.' That's not a purpose, that's a means to an end. *House Rich Cash Poor? No More!* is going to provide you with the tools to achieve that means to an end, but I hope and implore you to make it about much more in your life. Use this book as a tool to enable the kind of fulfilling life you dream of.

Without purpose, you will find yourself living what I call the default life. Default life is you on autopilot. You wake up, go to work, come home, eat dinner, watch television, go online, go to sleep, wake up, and repeat. Every day you go back to the job you dislike. But you keep going back because you are afraid of leaving. You don't know anything else. Before you know it, you will be 65, and will realize you've spent your entire working life, your entire career, being miserable. Oh, sure, there will have been a few happy moments, but you will have lived a mediocre default life. You probably didn't have the funds to travel the world. Perhaps you will have accumulated just enough to live frugally through your retirement until you die.

I'm amazed at how many people live each day without any sense of purpose or meaning. They go from day to day, just 'same stuff different day'. The same routines, the same outcomes, the same activities. I'm not saying there's anything wrong with routine, per se. But the question is: are your routines leading you to your purpose, to greater happiness, success, contentment, and results? The people who don't know what their purpose is are usually the ones who will fight and destroy each other. Life's routines have no particular meaning for them.

I hear and see this story over and over again, and I ask myself, "What was it all for?" Really. I mean, who did you save? Who did you bless? Who did you help? Who did you inspire? Who did you influence? What was the point of taking that time for yourself? How did you use your time? These may be some harsh questions, but the truth is that everyone here on this earth has a purpose. Even you. And it makes all the difference for you to find it and start living it. All we've got is time, only a finite amount of it, and we never know just how much time until it's gone. Why not make it count?

Your purpose is the path you follow during your journey through life. Your purpose is, by its very nature, something that you are passionate about. The mere thought of it gets your juices flowing. It drives your actions and motivates you, despite adversity and even the pain you might have to endure to reach it. The great achievers throughout history – Einstein, Napoleon, Martin Luther King, Oprah, Bob Marley, for example – each had a pretty clear purpose. The great ones throughout history believed in their purpose so passionately that some even died in the pursuit of it.

How about the Prime Minister of Canada? You can bet Justin Trudeau wakes up every morning with purpose. His purpose as Prime Minister when he won the 2015 election was to bring so-called sunny ways back to Canada's government. To bring leadership to a nation that is inherently inclusive, wise, generous, and respected around the world. Whether you agree with his politics is not the point. Justin Trudeau knows crucial decisions need to be made because he has a nation at home, and others around the world, depending on him, waiting for his direction. He conducts himself accordingly.

How would you feel about your purpose if you woke up tomorrow as the Prime Minister of Canada? Or maybe the President of the United States? How would you brush your teeth? What clothes would you put on? How would you walk? What decisions would you make? How long would it take you to make a decision? Would you eat better? Would you exercise more? Would you take better care of your body?

Are you living a purpose-driven life? If you are, great! If not, then you have work to do.

Your life purpose is not something you will find externally. Don't bother looking outside. Your purpose is not hiding somewhere outside of you, like a cruel game of hide and seek in the rocks and prickly bushes. It's internal, already inside of you.

We are all equipped with an internal compass to navigate the complexities of our physical reality. An inherent sense of what is right or wrong for us. The waypoints on this compass are your emotions. Your emotions will tell you whether you are at ease in a given situation, whether you are in the right place, whether others are being truthful, whether *you* are being truthful. Perhaps you can remember being a kid and questioning adult behaviour and demands that didn't make sense to you. Earlier still, as a newborn, you were completely in touch with who you were. You knew what you needed – food, comfort, or a diaper change. You were trusting and gave your love unconditionally. You acted from the truth of your inner compass, with no ego involved.

That inner compass is a sophisticated and valuable tool, once you know it is there and have learned to access it. From making difficult decisions regarding a moral dilemma to knowing how to treat others, your inner compass points toward the most energy efficient and effective response and course of action. Learn to trust your inner compass and it will inevitably guide you toward your best self. You need to engage your inner compass to reveal your purpose.

Eight Steps to Your Purpose

There are many different approaches to help you discover your life purpose. No one can figure this out for you or assign it to you. You must do your own work. Here are eight steps to help you discover your own unique purpose in life.

1. **Start a journal.** A journal is an excellent tool to employ in your purpose discovery program. You can journal in a notebook with good old fashioned paper and pen or you can journal online. This is the place to be honest with yourself. Write about your dreams, your desires, your thoughts.

2. **Get to know yourself.** Look inside. What are your core values? Everyone has a set of values, some sort of moral code that defines them. Your life purpose will honour these values. What do you believe about yourself? Do you know what your personality traits are, both great and not-so-great? What pushes your buttons? What brings you joy? What makes you happy?

3. **Identify your number one interest.** What's at the absolute top of the list for you? For inspiration, check the websites you've bookmarked, the books you read, the conversations you love to have with your friends. What do they all have in common? What are the things you love to do? These will be the things where time flies. "Whoa! It's four o'clock already?" And if you haven't ever found such a thing, it's time to get busy. Try new things. Take voice lessons. Backpack around Europe. Jump out of an airplane. Take a course. Experience. Discover.

4. **Inventory your experience, talents, and skills.** Not just the stuff on your resume, either. Look at what you do in your spare time. Ski? Knit? Sing? Build wooden boats? Think back to the stuff you used to do when you were young, too. Remember the baby's inner compass? Children and youth are often doing things they love and developing a skill or nurturing a talent. Did you love your piano lessons but haven't played as an adult? Add it to the list.

5. **Figure out how you want to impact the world.** This one is really important, because it provides the battery power for your internal compass. In what way do you want to make a positive difference in the world? This doesn't always have to be building something new, it can be dismantling something you believe is harmful or wrong. It might be educating people on a specific topic, changing laws to make the world a safer place, making sure the environment your kids and their kids grow up in is safer than today. Then you need to understand *why* this is how you impact the world.

6. **Keep an eye on what the world needs**. To really leverage your purpose, once you define it, you'll want to know how it fits with the global machine that is the world. You want to be generating income and supporting yourself in a way that is authentic to your purpose... so making sure there is actually a demand for what you want to offer is key. If you can't quite see a fit, then it might mean highlighting a different talent, or a different skill, in a slightly different way, while still authentically delivering on your life purpose.

7. **Hang around inspiring people.** Who are the people who inspire you? Who are the people already doing the things you are interested in? Get to know them. Learn from them. Ask them for advice. They won't be exactly like you, and they might not share your purpose, but if they're playing in your space, they've got value. Even if it is simply to share with you their journey to discovering their life purpose.

8. **Make friends with change.** Fear of change holds many people back from going after their life purpose. It's a misconception that sticking with the status quo is safe. If it keeps you from your life purpose, that is one of the biggest risks of all. You will be risking joy, fulfillment, achievement, happiness. Status quo – unless you're deliriously happy,

firing on all cylinders, helping the world, and living fully in your authentic life purpose – is a devil in disguise.

Discovering your life purpose takes some thought and introspection. Everyone is different when it comes to creating their purpose. Some are clear about it without having to give it a second thought. Others need guidance and support, from a friend, loved one, or coach to figure it out.

There's no wrong way to determine your unique purpose in life. If it takes work, so be it. The cost of not putting in the work is that you will always be controlled by external forces. But if you follow these steps, you'll be closer to fulfilling your life purpose.

You've Got Your Purpose. Now What?

Once you figure out your purpose, write it down. Write it on sticky notes and put it on the refrigerator, the bathroom mirror, your office wall, the dashboard of your car. Think about your purpose. Dream about it. Once you know your purpose, it is much easier to attract the money, the lifestyle, the wealth, the health, everything else that you want. It's like a magnet for your desires. But your life's work so far has likely littered the path with all sorts of roadblocks to your newly articulated life purpose. Here are the steps you can follow.

1. Analyze Your Current Situation

Analyze your current situation and look at the goals you are pursuing. Are you pursuing any? Why are you pursuing those goals? Do they align with your newly described life purpose? Are you on the path you're currently on because of the influence of something or somebody else? The people around us constantly pressure us to do things. Sometimes that's a good thing, but sometimes it's about doing things more favourable to them without benefit to us. I'm not talking about division of household chores here. Your partner obviously benefits if you clean the bathroom every Saturday. You may not enjoy doing that, but you benefit, too: you get a clean bathroom, and a happy partner. I'm talking about different things, bigger things. Things that change how you are in the world, how you see yourself, and how you feel about yourself. External pressures influence the personal decisions we all make. My point here is to recognize what those influences are, and assess them against how your resulting decisions align with your purpose. If they do align, great. Keep going. If they don't, what needs to change so you can be more authentic and fulfilled?

2. Work Toward Goals That Align With Your Purpose

With a clear idea of which goals will lead you to fulfill your purpose, which really means they give your life meaning, next you want to take steps toward achieving those goals. Continue pursuing these goals, knowing you will encounter roadblocks and objections and even failures. Keep your focus, chant your life purpose. Do whatever it takes to keep going.

Don't cave in to the expectations of other people or of society. I'm not suggesting you block out potentially important feedback. Use your inner compass to tell you whether you've encountered a legitimate reason to adjust your direction or your goal, or if someone else is simply trying to protect their territory. Trust that you know best what decisions to make and which actions to take to achieve the best life for yourself.

Life With Purpose

Some people are called to their purpose. Others accidentally uncover their purpose. Still others work hard to reveal it. There is no single best way, or best formula, for finding your purpose.

The key factors are:

1. the awareness that your purpose lies within you, not outside you, and
2. the commitment to find it, nurture it, and act on it.

Many wonderful changes happen once you discover your life purpose. You'll have greater focus in your daily activities. You'll have increased discipline with your daily productivity. You'll start racking up achievements. You'll feel passionate, motivated, and in control of your life. You'll find meaning and fulfillment more than you ever did before. Your energy and vitality will increase, you'll feel content and at peace. You'll feel an inner excitement about life, a kind of humming sensation inside your soul, because you know your place in the world and you know you're going to make it happen.

It doesn't matter whether you have a cynical personality; it doesn't matter if you've been living for 20, 30, 40 or more years with disinterest. When you discover and then live true to your life purpose, your soul will sing in a way you've never heard before. You'll realize that it isn't so much that anything is possible, but that it is possible to do anything that creates meaning for you.

Work, Money and Purpose

It's common for people to wish they had enough money so they could do whatever they want. They spend so much time on the 'wishing for money' thing that they never actually think about what it is that they want. By working out your purpose first, you will know what you want. You will be able to see, plan, and be inspired by it, and you will find the ways to create the money to get you where you want to be. If you've gotten this far and set a purpose that is only about finding, making and having money, you will have missed the point. It is not enough for your purpose to be just getting rich.

Financial freedom is an opportunity that everyone has, but very few people have the initiative, the drive, and the draw of a life purpose to achieve it. Your purpose is the thing that will drive you to accumulate wealth in a way that honours your purpose, as opposed to being contrary to it. For example, if your life purpose is to eliminate child labour and make children's lives better around the world, you won't be living true to your purpose if you run a mill in a third world country that employs child labour. Do you see my point?

It can work the other way around, too. Until you've defined your purpose, your business or your work may seem like drudgery. You've got no broader purpose, no reason or meaning to get up every day and go to the job.

Here's an example. A couple of people I know run a handyman business. I'll call them Joe and Bill. They were trudging along, stuck on the work-to-pay-bills treadmill. Joe and Bill were in debt, barely getting by, and growing less and less motivated to keep working at their business.

One evening they attended a seminar that helped them reveal their life purpose. Suddenly it became clear that the business was the vehicle that was going to *fund* that purpose. This put a whole new shine on what had previously become old and dull. They began to see what was possible to achieve if their business was successful. They changed what they'd been doing. They raised prices and limited the jobs they'd accept to only those large jobs that were profitable. They subcontracted out some of their work to increase productivity.

Suddenly, the business was booked six months in advance. The debt was paid off and the cash flowing in was channeled to more than just paying the bills: it was now funding their purpose.

Your Definite Purpose

To become financially free and able to achieve your life purpose, you must find a way to fund the journey. It's a fact of life. The method that you choose to fund your journey is called your *definite purpose*. And a person with a definite purpose is a person with the focus, intent, and desire to reach his/her ultimate goals.

What's the business model you will use to create that wealth? When you figure that out, that model must become your mission in life. Everything you do from that point forward is geared toward reaching your ultimate goal: living your life purpose and attaining financial freedom.

This definite purpose should be desirable enough for you to tackle your life purpose with all your energy and effort. You must wake up excited about working and you must go to sleep thinking about it. Once you start on this path, one of the fundamental laws of the universe kicks in to help you.

The law I'm talking about is 'like attracts like'. When you start working on your definite purpose on the road to your life purpose, every cell in your body and mind will be working together, in unison, to help you. You will attract other people in your life that you can use to form a team. You will see opportunities where there were none before. It just happens. It's a fundamental law of the universe. Yes, I said it again on purpose. It's a fundamental law of the universe.

Once you've discovered your true purpose, you'll find it becomes easier to say no to barriers that would otherwise get in the way of your definite purpose or your life purpose. It will be easier to turn down invitations that might cause you to miss a deadline or temptations to spend money on unnecessary items that erode your progress toward financial freedom. You'll say no because you can see so clearly what you're working towards that you're motivated not to stray.

If you are not in touch or in tune with your true purpose – your true motivation or reason for being, doing and living - then you are leaving the outcome to chance. You are leaving your destiny in the hands of others. Someone else will control your career, your decisions, and your destination.

Destination Vs Destiny

Don't be confused about destination versus destiny. Your destiny is not predetermined by anything or anyone except you. Accepting a mediocre life as your destiny is simply a lame excuse for an unwillingness to take responsibility. That may sound harsh, but it's true. You, and you alone, control and create your destiny every day with the decisions you make and the actions you take. Simple as that.

With a clear purpose, you'll create your own destiny and attach it to your decisions and actions with conviction and desire. You'll be doing what you are good at and the people you influence will reap the benefits of your gift. You might not be rich right away, and you'll need to watch your spending, but you'll have enough coming in to cover your expenses and a bit leftover to splurge.

With a clear purpose, your livelihood and sense of self aren't tied to a particular job, title, or position. When your thoughts, words and actions are aligned with your purpose, and you live from a space of inner harmony, this is freedom.

With a clear purpose, things change in your mind. There will be a reason behind everything you do. You will enjoy a clarity of focus about everything in your life and decisions will come more easily.

You will find you *want* to pay off those credit cards instead of buying a new pair of shoes. You'll *want* to clear up your debts and loans instead of buying a new truck. Soon you'll be investing and creating cash flow. You'll have extra money at the end of the month. You'll realize you're right in front of your purpose. That's the feeling. You will be able to embrace it and walk in it.

With your purpose, and with this book, you will have everything you need to put your money to work *for you,* and not the other way around.

> *It's not the things we do in life that we regret on our deathbed. It is the things we do not.*

— RANDY PAUSCH

* * *

3

CREDIT AND CREDIT SCORE

Y ou can be forgiven if you've racked up credit card debt on top of car loans, maybe on top of a student loan, and, of course, on top of the mortgage. Everybody does it. As well as a spending society, ours is a consumer-debt-driven society. In the name of keeping the economy humming, we are all urged to spend, spend, spend, borrow, borrow, borrow. Instant gratification on steroids, with 'get it now and don't pay for 24 months' marketing campaigns that convince us it's okay to get something for nothing, or at least to get something for nothing now and pay more for it later.

The central banks set interest rates based on what is required to keep consumers like you and me spending – and borrowing. The lower the interest rate, the higher household debt grows. Just look at Canada. For the first time ever, consumer debt in 2016 in Canada was greater than the country's gross domestic product (GDP). And it's not just banks that have consumers drinking the credit Kool-Aid. Credit card companies are in the debt game too. They don't want you to pay off your balance every month; they are alive and thriving because of the millions who carry balances one month to the next.

Maybe you remember your grandparents' saving strategy of stashing their hard-earned money under the mattress and paying only cash for purchases. Sorry, Grandma. Car dealerships don't want you to walk in and pay cash for that new car, because then they'd miss out on the administration fees you pay to process your zero-down, uber-low interest rate car loan.

The pressure and practice of relying on debt starts early. Kids learn it from their parents. University students borrow for tuition and living expenses, often relying on credit cards to keep them in Kraft Dinner and beer. In the lobby or hallway of each hallowed institution, on the first day or the first week of each new semester, there they are. The predators: the people who sign up the young, excited, impressionable youths with their first credit cards, connecting them to their first addictive taste of debt. Books are expensive, tuition is high, and beer isn't cheap. The trap is that students believe the credit card is a saving grace, an answered prayer of independence. Instead, it's often the first shackle in a lifetime chained to the unrelenting trap of debt.

Despite promises to handle the credit card wisely and with care, very few either keep that promise or know what it means. Racking up balances on these credit cards is fast and easy with a busy student life, where so much is new, expectations are high, and being financially responsible is not yet a skill. And the next thing you know, that student is faced with more debt than they can possibly handle. By this point, you probably can't even remember what you bought with that credit card. It's gone.

Do you recognize this scenario? Did I just describe your young adulthood introduction to credit cards? So, what do you do? For starters, you get a job immediately after graduation because you have all this debt hanging over your head and you need to find the means to pay it off. Any job will do. It doesn't have to be your dream job, it just has to help you attack the pressure of debt.

I'm not advocating you don't ever use credit. You should. In fact, I lay out a detailed plan for quickly paying down mortgage debt in chapter seven, 'Leveraging Equity', and using a credit card plays a key role. But you must understand how it can benefit you, and stop using credit in a way that hurts you. Debt is a four-letter word. But it's not all bad. Knowing how to use debt to your advantage, which debts to pay off and which ones to carry, can literally save you thousands of dollars. That's money you can put to work for you by investing in new opportunities.

Credit Ratings

Our economy is set up on a system that honours a good credit rating almost more than any other trait. You can be a good and kind human being who does generous things for other people. But if your credit rating or score sucks, you may have some work to do as you travel on the road to financial success. Yet, as important as your credit rating is to your quality of life and financial health, very few people know what their credit score is.

In fact, it's likely you can recall your social insurance number or the phone number of your high school sweetheart, but you don't know the number of your credit score. Yet this seemingly innocuous number has the power to control your life in ways that might surprise you. The three digit score you're assigned by the credit bureaus can be the deciding factor between whether you get the car, the house, or even the job of your dreams. It's that important.

Here's how it works. Every company that extends credit to you reports your reliability on making payments and overall debt load to central credit bureaus. And I do mean every company. It's the cell-phone service provider that extends credit in the form of phone and web browsing services and bills you monthly. It's the credit card company that gives you a card you can use to purchase discretionary items. Or it's the retailer that sells you a car or home theatre system, exchanging the right to take the item home today for an agreed future repayment schedule and rate of interest.

These companies, big and small, that in one way or another extend you credit, report all your payment history to the credit bureaus. Even if you have a perfect payment record and you are late by just one day on just one payment, it is a black mark and it becomes part of your credit history.

How the Rating Agencies Work

The credit bureau gathers all these company reports, assembles the data, and applies some kind of secret mathematical formula to assign you a three-digit numerical credit score. The two largest companies that do this in Canada are Equifax and TransUnion. In addition, these companies often give you an overall credit rating, which differs slightly from a credit score. Confusing? You bet.

You may think you are doing all the right things to protect your financial health: consolidating your debts, closing bank accounts and credit cards you use very little or not at all, even working hard to pay off your mortgage. But you'd be wrong, which can seem even more mind boggling. These assumed good habits can actually hurt your credit score. Really confused now? Well, I'm here to explain why and to help you use and manage your credit better in a way that protects your credit score.

Credit Score

Your credit score is a judgment about your financial health at a specific point in time. It indicates the risk you represent for lenders compared with other consumers. While lenders consider many factors, including income, when making credit decisions, your credit score is at the top of their list.

Let's say you're in the market for credit and your lender of choice determines, largely based on your credit score, that you are very low risk. This may open the door to higher credit limits on credit cards and the lowest interest rates on loans. If you are applying for a mortgage, an excellent credit score can help you secure the best interest rate, often saving you literally tens of thousands of dollars over the term of your mortgage. That's money you've freed up to invest elsewhere.

So, if you're in the majority of consumers who don't know their credit score, it's time to take off the blinders and get real about the state of your financial health.

There are many different ways to work out credit scores. The credit reporting agencies use three-digit numerical scores from 300 to 900. High scores on this scale are good. The higher your score, the lower the risk for lenders, the lower the interest rate they'll offer you, and the more they'll lend.

The best scores are over 750. A score between 700 and 749 is considered very good. Between 650 and 699 is bankable good credit. Between 600 and 649 are not quite as good but mortgages are still possible. Anything below 600 means you may want to seek alternative sources of financing and your score could use some attention.

It's worth noting only 27 per cent of the population scores between 750 and 799, but that's a good range to aim for. Statistically only two per cent of borrowers in this category will default on a loan or go bankrupt in the next few years. Those are figures lenders know they can bank on.

A score below 750 is still a good score and lenders will love you. The general cut-off number, again, is below 600. You probably won't be approved for that loan for the fiery red little sports car, or anything else, from traditional conservative lenders like the banks. There are lenders who play in the lower credit score space, but do expect to pay a higher interest rate.

What's in a Credit Score?

Most credit bureaus use a variation of the same formula to calculate your credit score. Here's how the five components of the formula are broken down, at the time of this writing.

- Your payment history makes up 35 per cent of the score. This element relates to factors such as your record of paying on time.
- Credit utilization is set at 30 per cent. Credit utilization is the ratio of your credit card balance to your credit limit. For example, if your balance is $200 and your credit limit is $1,000, your credit utilization on that card is 20 per cent. The lower this number is, the better. You should aim for balances under 30 per cent. Any credit card balances above 50 per cent of your limit will hurt your score.
- The length of your credit history accounts for 15 per cent of the formula. In basic terms, lenders feel more comfortable with a borrower with an established credit history. This is where the 'don't close old accounts' advice comes in to play. Especially if you're about to make a loan application.
- The final 20 per cent of the formula puzzle includes any new

credit, which accounts for 10 per cent, and the types of credit used, also factored in at 10 per cent.

- These figures are then combined in some secret mathematical formula and, voila, your three-digit credit score emerges.

Factors That Harm Your Credit Score

I've already mentioned a few factors that harm your credit score, such as missing or late payments, balances over 50 per cent of your credit card limit, and closing old bank accounts or credit cards. But here are a few more to consider. Did you know having too many or too few accounts is a problem? But nobody seems to know how many are too many or too few. Carrying loan balances too high compared with the original loan can hurt you, too. Keep in mind, the longer it takes you to pay off that loan, no matter how small, the more your score is negatively affected. And be careful about applying for too many credit cards or loans within a 12-month period. Do you really need that department store credit card that's offered to you at the checkout counter just to save 20 per cent on a one-time bill? Be judicious with how many credit cards you really need. And every time a lender or business checks your credit, your file takes a hit.

Your lifestyle matters, too. Like how long you stay at one address (hint: the longer, the better) and how often you change jobs. Lenders want stability.

Now, here comes the whopper, the head-shaker, the one factor that can drag your credit score down in the gutter. The one thing that on the surface makes absolutely no sense. Having no debt is really bad for your credit score. Let that sink in. Having no debt means there is nothing on your file to show lenders you are good for the money. There is no payment history, no credit utilization, nothing for lenders to spin in their magical formula machine. This means you may be the most trustworthy person, the most responsible money manager on the planet, but you can't prove it. So, forget paying off all your debts and closing the accounts. You are better off keeping credit cards, especially old ones, and using them at least once in a while. Pay off the balance in total every month, if you can. If you must keep a balance, be sure to make your payments on time.

I know what you're thinking: this means you will pay interest on the balance. True. So, keep balances low. At least you'll have an excellent credit score. You will need it for those big purchase items like a loan for a car or a mortgage for a house.

Remember earlier when I hinted that paying off your mortgage may not be the smartest move if you're hoping to get an A on your financial report card? Here's why. As soon as you pay off your mortgage, that reporting account is removed from your file and you are effectively placed in the unknown category. This means you will have points removed from your credit score. Seems unfair, doesn't it? (All the more reason to use the equity in your home, keep a balance on your mortgage, and put your money to work for you. We'll get to that in more detail shortly.)

But look on the bright side. An excellent credit score will secure you the best low interest rate on your mortgage, which can mean huge savings over the term of your loan. So, do what you can to keep your credit score high.

Bad credit can cost you more than a loan or mortgage. It can also cost you your dream job if prospective employers ask to see your credit file. Let this be your credit motto: keep your balances low and your limits high.

Liane and Jeff's Credit Story

My clients Liane and Jeff experienced a situation that demonstrates the power of a bad credit score. They were going through some tough times financially and in an effort to stay in their home and avoid having to move their kids, took out a second mortgage. They used the proceeds of the second mortgage to do some renovations, replace the roof, and take the kids on a week-long vacation to Disney World in Florida. The kids loved it.

It wasn't long after they returned from that holiday that they started having trouble keeping up with the first mortgage, second mortgage, utility bills, property taxes, car payment, credit card payments, and the other expenses that always come along with raising a family. And then, to make matters worse, Jeff had a minor accident at work, which meant he had to take six weeks of sick time. Granted, he had health coverage from his employer that thankfully provided almost two-thirds of his regular salary. But Jeff and Liane's budget was already bursting at the seams, and this little incident and the accompanying reduction in take-home pay put them over the top.

They decided to downsize. They would sell their home and buy something much smaller and more manageable financially. They tried to remain optimistic that they'd find something in a neighbourhood they liked just as much and did not want their kids to have to change schools. So, they cleaned, painted, and listed their home. In a matter of days, they had a solid offer from a prospective buyer. While they were signing the paperwork to accept the offer, Liane called me.

"David, we're going to be in the market for a new mortgage," Liane said over the phone. "We're selling the property and are going to downsize to free up some room in our budget. We're signing papers with the buyer now."

I'd been working with Liane and Jeff long enough to have a pretty good idea what their situation was and how their situation had impacted their credit score.

"That's great," I said. "So, your credit score is repaired and you won't have trouble putting at least 20 per cent down?"

I heard a swift intake of air, then silence.

Liane and Jeff had forgotten about their credit score. Through their struggles, they'd been late on a few payments, missed a couple of others, and their debt load was maxed. Their resulting credit score meant they'd be ineligible for any mortgage without at least 20 per cent down. In the Toronto market and with their other debt load, that was going to be impossible. They proceeded with the sale of their home regardless, as they didn't feel they had much choice.

In my office a few weeks later, Liane was in tears. They both had deteriorated credit scores and were not going to be able to get another mortgage to buy another home. Even finding a rental home with their credit score was a problem. This was a setback they hadn't counted on.

Had they called me before putting their home on the market, we could have developed a strategy to manage cash flow, repair their score, and make downsizing to another home as owners a smoother transition.

It wasn't all bad news. I was able to help Liane and Jeff get into a new home with my rent-to-own program. We'll get to that program in more detail in chapter six, 'Home Ownership'.

Credit Rating Scale

You've likely heard of a credit rating more often than a credit score. For the most part, credit ratings are used to assess the financial health of businesses rather than individuals. But when a credit rating is assigned to rate your personal credit, the lender uses a single digit rating scale of zero to nine.

With this scale, one of two letters precede the number. 'I' indicates instalment credit like a mortgage or car loan and 'R' stands for revolving credit such as credit cards. The most common ratings are revolving credit or 'R' ratings. The numeric scale of one to nine indicates how many months late you are in paying. A rating of the number one (1) is as good as it gets. So, an R1 rating means you pay all your bills within 30 days of the due date. R2 means you paid in more than 30 days from the due date but not more than 60 days. If it had been more than 60 days, you would get an R3 and so on. If you've missed several of your Visa payments, you may get an R5.

What you really don't want to ever see is a nine. A rating of R9 means you are a write-off, or at least your loan is, because you never paid it back. Usually an R9 is reserved for debts that are placed in collection or bankruptcy. Unlike the numbers of your credit score, in the ratings game the lower the number, the better.

Credit Report

You know the importance of getting an annual physical exam. You might not like it, but it's necessary for maintaining good health and it just might save your life if a problem is detected and corrected early. The same thinking should be applied to your financial health. I highly recommend you get an annual credit report and financial review. Your credit report comes from the credit rating agencies. You can also schedule a financial review with me at davidrhodd.com.

A credit report is a report card on your financial health. It lists a history of your payments, what types of credit you have, and how much credit you are using. It's the information ratings agencies evaluate to calculate the numbers in the secret credit score formula.

More than 21 million Canadians have credit reports on file with the credit bureaus, yet most of us have no idea what's in them. It is your right to know what is being tracked and reported about your credit and finances. It can be the difference between getting that important loan or mortgage or repeatedly being denied credit. It's not a flimsy document either. It is loaded with personal information, including every loan you've taken out, whether you pay on time, how much you owe on each credit card, and what your limits are. It also provides a list of every lender who has accessed your file. It's got your birthdate, every address you've called home since you got your first credit extension, and key identification information like your social insurance number.

Basically, it is like Big Brother watching your every credit transaction.

For this reason alone, it is even more shocking that most North Americans don't know what's in their own credit reports. If you've ever been denied credit and don't know why, chances are the answer is in your credit report. Get it. And then make sure you check it over very carefully for any errors or discrepancies.

How to Get Your Credit Report

Your credit report is an open book on your credit health and history, and precautions are taken to make sure it ends up in the right hands – either yours only or those to whom you've given explicit permission. In Canada, a credit report is called a credit file disclosure by Equifax Canada and a consumer disclosure by TransUnion Canada. You can get your file free of charge if you order by mail, fax, or telephone. You must be able to receive it by mail or in person. If you want to get your credit file right away, there is a fee to access it online.

To order by mail or fax, make your request in writing using the documents provided by Equifax Canada and TransUnion Canada. You will need copies of two pieces of authorized identification. Or you can order by telephone using the automated system provided by the credit reporting agencies. For this ordering method, you will need to confirm your identity by answering a series of personal questions and provide both your social insurance number (SIN) and/or a credit card number. Once you have your credit report in hand, look it over very carefully.

Errors in Your Credit Report

You might be surprised to know that there's a fair chance there are mistakes in your file. The sheer volume of items listed with credit reporting agencies means mistakes are likely, if not inevitable. On average, up to 33 per cent of files contain inaccuracies. Some can be serious enough to hurt your credit status, resulting in a denied loan or a higher interest rate. Make sure your file isn't one of them. The credit bureaus accept all these tidbits of information on you from your creditors via electronic means. They put everything in your file without checking if the information is true. That's not their job. But it is their responsibility to respond and investigate any complaint you make about your own file. Some common mistakes to watch for include an incorrect mailing address or social insurance number, late payments where you know – and can prove – you've been on time, and any unauthorized inquiries on your file. Some of these errors could be signs of identity theft, so it's very important you check and verify all the information in your file at least annually.

If you do spot an error, contact the credit bureau. It will investigate your complaint and contact the reporting creditor to verify the information it filed with the reporting agency. The creditor then has to verify the item it placed on your file and you are entitled to be part of the process. Check again within 30 to 60 days after disputing errors. If any errors remain, contact the creditor yourself directly to see if it can be taken off your credit profile. Be diligent. Tell your side of the story in a consumer statement that is added to your file.

How Your Credit Score is Used

Every time you apply for credit – from an Internet service provider, for hydro electricity, cable television, any sort of loan, a credit card, or a mortgage – the extending party will access your credit rating from the rating agency. It uses the information to judge whether you're worth taking a risk on. Will you pay? Will you pay on time? Whenever you rent or lease an apartment or other property, you can expect your prospective landlord to check into your credit score before deciding whether you get the keys. Your credit score can make the difference between home and heartache.

This is the stage where you need to flip that switch. Use credit, but use it wisely. Pay attention to the extra money you're leaving on the table when you continually carry balances that result in sometimes exorbitant interest payments. Keep your balances well below your credit limit. Check your credit score and history at least annually. By doing this, you will create room for savings, and you'll be ready to make your money work better for you. Stay tuned, because I will soon tell you how to leverage the room you're creating in your credit limits to build wealth.

* * *

4

CASH FLOW – DEBT LOW – TAX NO

"You will never know true freedom until you achieve financial freedom."

— ROBERT KIYOSAKI

The basic principle of making your money work for you, and not the other way around, is to have more money coming in than going out. Achieving this is about ditching the default life, paying down your debts, increasing your cash flow without necessarily increasing your efforts, and paying less tax.

Where Does the Money Go?

Some days there just doesn't seem to be enough money to go around, right? Before you can do anything to change your financial situation, you need to know where your income goes. Of course, you have day-to-day expenses. Everybody does. We all must eat, wear clothes, have somewhere to sleep, and more. These are facts of life. But there are many other demands on your money. Those who are financially successful have learned that some ways of spending money bring more value than others. Being wealthy is not simply about having a higher salary. It's about what you do with your money.

Being cash poor often involves spending too much money on things that depreciate or even disappear entirely. Of course, some of these things are necessities, so I'm not saying that poor people are to blame for being poor. I am saying that spending too much on things takes money away from potentially fruitful outlets and wastes it in unfruitful ones.

People who are in the middle class often own one big asset – a home – and must continue working to pay for it and their other expenses. Much of their worth is locked inside that single asset.

Wealthy people buy multiple assets that will appreciate. They invest money to earn more money and find creative but legitimate ways to reduce their taxes. This approach can bring the most freedom and the most cash flow.

A Partnership Affair

Managing cash flow and making financial decisions is best handled in partnership with your spouse. You might be surprised how many couples are still locked in the '50s-era model of handling the finances: it's a job for him, not her. If this describes how you and your partner divvy up household tasks, I implore you to make a change. And if you're single now, remember this when you enter into your next relationship. It's not just about gender equality. It's about practicality, security, and common sense.

When I was introduced to Kama, she was distraught and overwhelmed. During her 25-plus year marriage to her husband Hiromi, he always handled all of the finances. Hiromi made a lot of money in construction, which he'd invested in a diverse international portfolio.

They owned a restaurant which Kama happily ran. Kama never had to worry about the money, ever. Until Hiromi had a stroke and became bedridden and unable to communicate.

She was in tears during our first meeting, and again in our second. She'd tried to manage on her own for months, but bills were piling up, the house needed some major repairs, and she hadn't a clue how to access their significant investment portfolio or insurance policies when she needed to.

I taught her about the basics: how and when to pay each of her monthly utility bills, how to keep mortgage and debt payments on time to protect her credit score, and how to balance her cheque book. She was 52 and she had never been exposed to any of the most basic money management concepts.

There's no way to predict when or to whom a health issue or worse will arise. Sharing the money management of the household from the start is a way to demonstrate caring for your partner. So that if something happens to either of you, you both already know what to do.

I worked with Kama to identify where all the investments were. I helped her determine which home repairs were most important and I helped her arrange and hire contractors. The house was huge – six bedrooms, two levels, a massive yard. It was big for two people, and even bigger when one of the two became incapacitated. The other was trying to learn the ropes in a hurry, while still managing day-to-day operation of the restaurant. Even though her husband had earned an excellent living and invested well, the sudden loss of his income put a serious chill on the state of Kama's cash flow. Things were going south in a hurry, and it was serious by the time I got involved.

Kama moved into one of the bedrooms for several months while renting out the main floor of her home to generate some extra cash.

We worked together to pull equity out of the home to fix it up and ready it for sale. Once the home sold, Kama bought a very nice two-bedroom condo for herself and Hiromi that was much easier for her to manage on her own. There were enough proceeds from the sale of the home that Kama could afford to invest some back into the restaurant. She upgraded her ordering and payroll systems, spruced up the customer seating area, and upgraded some appliances. Hiromi still lives with Kama, but requires round-the-clock care.

My client relationship with Kama was an unusual one in that it required me to become intimately familiar with every single financial detail in her life, no matter how small. The result, with Kama now comfortably back on track and settled down, is that our relationship is more of a friendship. I regularly drop by the restaurant with my family for a meal. Kama makes a big fuss and we catch up on what's been happening in our lives.

And she still calls me when she needs a recommendation for a plumber.

Kama and Hiromi's Debt

Without Hiromi's income, and without knowing how their money worked, Kama's debt had quickly become a problem. It got in the way of her ability to manage the restaurant, which had suddenly become their only source of income.

For many people, it is difficult to generate strong cash flow while they are saddled with a high level of debt. In this case, the first step is to reduce that debt.

I'm about to share with you my surefire method for cash flow planning and paying down debt. But first, a note about my choice of the phrase 'cash flow planning' and not 'budgeting'. There's a big difference.

When you budget, you are setting a ceiling on the income you have to work with and all your focus is on keeping your spending below this amount. It's like setting up a limiting belief. This is not a mindset likely to lead you to financial freedom.

Cash flow planning, on the other hand, keeps the notion open that if you find you do not have enough income to accomplish what you want, you have room to figure out how to increase that side of the ledger. It's not always about reducing expenses.

Here's the surefire method to use for cash flow planning and paying down debt.

1. Know how much money comes in.

Don't make the mistake of thinking that your gross salary represents the money you have to work with. That thinking must change. Your gross salary figure may be used to help a bank or mortgage lender determine how large a loan you qualify for, but otherwise it is a number you should banish from your brain. Figure out what your after-tax income is and let that number stick. We will discuss taxes later in this chapter, so for now just determine the dollars that actually arrive in your hands each month.

2. Know exactly how much money goes out.

Write down your fixed expenses and tally them up. They will fall into two main categories: fixed expenses and discretionary expenses. Fixed expenses include your mortgage repayments, rent, car payments, mobile phone bills, utility bills, basic groceries, transportation, daycare, school fees, and so on. (Although everything is discretionary, you can choose what kind of car to drive and choose one that doesn't require a loan payment, only maintenance. You can restrict your smartphone usage – gasp! – to reduce your cell phone bill. You get the picture.) Discretionary expenses include everything else: those coffees you buy at Tim Hortons or Starbucks, lunch with workmates, new clothes, extra groceries beyond the basics, tickets to the movies or sporting events, and so on.

3. Write down all your due dates on one calendar.

Expenses, bills, and repayments can fall on many different dates. Keep careful track of them so you can plan accordingly and not forget any due dates. Missing one hurts your credit score, remember? It might mean curtailing your spending over one weekend if you know you've got a bill due Monday and you don't get paid until next Friday.

4. Limit your discretionary expenses and stick to it.

Do not borrow against next month's income by going over the spending limits in your cash flow plan. That's a recipe for mounting credit card debt and will spoil the entire system.

5. Track every penny you spend for at least 30 days.

Yes, this requires diligence and discipline. It is worth it. You will learn exactly where your money is going. Most people who do this exercise end up at least a little surprised. You'll quickly learn the value of each dollar, how expenses add up, and what expenses are worthwhile. You may also notice patterns that tell you where and why your money seems to be disappearing.

6. Start paying down your debts. One at a time.

When it comes to paying down debts, there are several approaches out there. Look at the ones that produce the best results. Paying a little into each debt (car loan, credit cards, store credit, line of credit, etc.) and trying to steadily reduce them all at the same time is a recipe for taking much longer and paying more interest, regardless of how much sense it might seem to make. Instead, pay off one debt at a time.

Decide whether it will cost less for you to pay off the smallest debt balance first or the one with the highest interest rate. Maybe roll several smaller debts into one and attack that aggressively. And whatever you do, stop creating additional debt.

7. Seek professional debt help if you need it.

If you are still struggling to reduce your debt levels, especially if you live in fear of not having enough income to pay all your commitments, approach professional services for debt counselling and management. Get it paid down as effectively as possible to free you up to really get going on the road to financial freedom.

In the end, the key is to know exactly how much money you have coming in and going out. You need to write down everything, track it all, and be sure your income is always higher than the amount going out.

If you'd like some help running your numbers, you can always hop over to davidrhodd.com, book a consultation, and I or someone on my team will be happy to talk you through it.

But a word of caution about financial advisors: I recommend you stick to fee-only financial planners, because that means *you* are paying *them* to act in your best interests. If *you* pay no fees, then *someone else* is paying them to act in their best interest. Your money is too important to let someone else's priorities take precedence over your own.

8. Bring in more.

Keep your cash flow planning mindset active and always look for opportunities to create extra cash flow at the end of each month. Whether this is buying fewer coffees, committing to bring your lunch four out of five days every week, taking a bus instead of a cab, working an extra shift or even an extra job on the side, there are always ways to cut expenses or increase income.

9. Investigate alternative tools.

Paper and pencil work fine for cash flow planning and budget reduction plans, but there are many other alternative tools out there that make the task easier, and even enjoyable.

For example, I hold the license for a proprietary software that will enhance your cash flow planning and help you reach your goals faster. Reach out to me via davidrhodd.com for more information and I'll be happy to help.

Cash Flow

"Success is a poor teacher... Remember that anything important can't really be learned in the classroom. It must be learned by taking action, making mistakes, and then correcting them. That's when wisdom sets in."

— ROBERT T. KIYOSAKI.

Let me help you follow where your money is going so you can have better cash flow. I will briefly walk you through a system that outlines the differences between assets and liabilities, along with the differences between what wealthier people teach their children about money and what poorer and middle class parents teach. I follow two of Robert Kiyosaki's main ideas, which are to become more educated and literate about finance, and to use investing and entrepreneurship to determine your financial future and freedom.

Kiyosaki wrote a second book entitled *Cashflow Quadrant: Rich Dad's Guide to Financial Freedom*. It is this concept of cash flow that can help you reduce your debts and understand how to generate money and income from sources other than work. (I use 'cash flow' as two words even though the title of Kiyosaki's book uses 'cashflow'.)

Kiyosaki's cash flow quadrant looks like this.

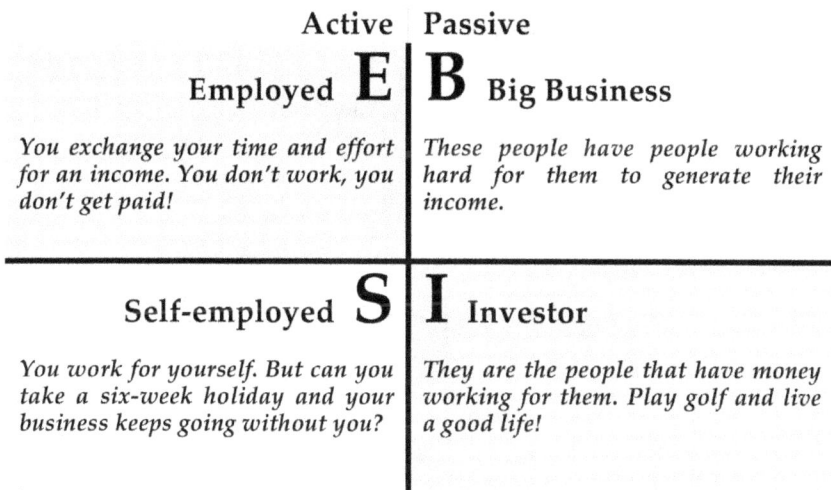

Active	Passive
Employed E	B **Big Business**
You exchange your time and effort for an income. You don't work, you don't get paid!	*These people have people working hard for them to generate their income.*
Self-employed S	I **Investor**
You work for yourself. But can you take a six-week holiday and your business keeps going without you?	*They are the people that have money working for them. Play golf and live a good life!*

People, their finances, and business dealings fit into one or more of those four areas. Some people reside in one quadrant, sometimes two, while others may progress through all four quadrants as they move through different stages of their lives.

It is possible for a person to fit into multiple quadrants, sometimes all of them, but most people fit one only.

On the left side are the quadrants 'E' for Employee and 'S' for Self-employed. On the right are the quadrants 'I' for Investor and 'B" for Business Owner.

Note that E and S are on the left side of the graph (the 'active income' side) while B and I are on the right ('passive income'). That is because there is a significant divide between them. Active income requires you to be present and involved all the time. Passive income does not. You can still make money even when you're not working.

E – Employee

You have a job. Most people belong in this area only and they essentially start each day at zero because no work means no money.

Working for a company is essentially trading time for money. Making more money involves either finding a better paying job or working more hours. There is no passive income.

S – Self-employed

This entails some more financial and personal freedoms in daily life from a regular job, but it is still trading time and effort for money.

B – Business Owner

You personally don't have to be working all the time to make the business generate income because you have employees. You trade products or services (instead of your time) for money.

I – Investor

This is where money really works for you, rather than vice versa. Cash flow and passive income come from investments. They involve the least time investment and produce long-term revenue.

Figure out where you currently fit on the graph. From where do you receive most of your income? Where you fit can be influenced and changed by your stage of life, your approach, your outlook, your values, and your actions. Next, decide where you want to be.

My advice is to move toward the B and I side where passive income dominates. Your goal should be to seek financial independence and there is a higher probability of achieving that success if you are in the Investor and/or Business Owner quadrants.

Kama and Hiromi were mainly in the B and I quadrants, but managing the restaurant meant Kama also had one foot firmly in the S quadrant. There is nothing wrong with being on the active income side as an employee or self-employed person. You can still achieve financial independence and start to become wealthy, but it often takes more time and effort. As an employee or self-employed individual, you are tied to specific systems and rules that may not leave you with monthly disposable income.

True financial freedom is more self-sustaining. To move from one quadrant to another requires a significant paradigm shift and change in values, outlook, and daily routine. When you retire, for example, these kinds of changes take place and you will move to the passive income side. But you get to decide if you want to be on that side sooner.

It is not so much about the road less travelled. Take the path that offers you better opportunities.

Be Financially Savvy: Ditch the Default Life

"People think that working hard for money and then buying things that make them look rich will make them rich. In most cases it doesn't. It only

makes them more tired. They call it 'Keeping up with the Joneses'. And if you notice, the Joneses are exhausted."

— ROBERT T. KIYOSAKI

As an employee, you are subject to what I called the default life in chapter two, 'Find Your Purpose Within'. Here, life is predictable. You go on autopilot, following the same daily routine of going to work, paying bills, and paying taxes. It's like a 1950s movie, although today's salaries rarely provide the comfortable and spacious homes depicted on screen.

The default life also makes taxes predictable and routine. A set level of income equals a set amount of taxes to pay. A set amount of taxes means there is a set amount of take home pay left over. And a certain amount of take home pay equals a particular standard of living. Have you ever noticed that most employees seem to have only just enough at the end of each month? Or maybe they don't have enough, because they spend more than they plan and they have to scrounge or borrow to get by until next payday. In reality, just enough means just above broke.

Sure, you can increase your income, but to do that you must give up more of your time and energy. You either have to work over-time or put in more hours to generate opportunities for bonuses. Then, when you increase your income, you are responsible for paying more taxes. Working hard to earn more money and then giving it to the tax man is not the way to get ahead, even if you do manage to save some for retirement. It is hardly worth devoting more of your time to a system like this. It reminds me of a hamster on a wheel, just going round and round. Extra effort produces more speed, but for no real net result. With no offence to the hamster, this is actually the rat race. You are in a cycle of paying a high interest rate on credit cards, carrying other debts, dealing with taxes, adjusting your cash flow plan for price increases, and the list continues.

It is time to break this cycle for something far better. It can be a difficult cycle to break unless you uncover the clear and focused intention – your purpose. Find your purpose in life and then learn how to make your money work hard for you. Do what you can to move yourself to the B (business) and I (investor) quadrants. You will pay less tax and have more for achieving your goals.

Becoming Financial Educated

To move from the active income side of Kiyosaki's quadrant graph to the passive income side requires you to learn about financial dealings. The rules inside each quadrant are very different. With knowledge can come the freedom to control your destiny.

Be prepared to take what you may currently think are risks. They seem like risks only if you are not familiar with them or don't understand how they work. Move from thinking about job security to owning your financial freedom.

Of course, that is not to say there are no risks involved, especially if you create or buy your own business or invest your money in stocks and shares. A high percentage of new businesses fail in their first five years (but not the 80 per cent many people say). Do not let fear infect your thinking and dreaming. Fear limits potential.

Learn from the failures of others, listen to those who have achieved success, and develop the skills you need. You will not learn enough (or anything) in school about how to gain financial freedom or be a business owner or investor. You must be curious with an appetite to learn. Read books, take courses, converse with experts, and weigh options and approaches.

Then be true to the purpose and mission you have set for yourself. The rewards that await you can be great.

The Tax Trap

I was reading an article a couple of years ago that said the average Canadian was taxed at 42 per cent of their total income. There is income tax, GST, fuel tax, food taxes, and more. A significant proportion of every dollar earned can be removed in taxes and whatever remains must go toward housing, clothing, insurance, debt payments, and more. After paying your taxes, you realize you do not have much left at all the end of the month. So, you resort to credit cards to fill the gap, which leads you to pay an interest rate of about 25 per cent, sometimes more. This is, of course, in addition to your mortgage, and on a $400,000 mortgage over 25 years you will end up paying more than $200,000 in interest. Looking at the long-term picture, with that $400,000 mortgage plus the interest, you need to earn significantly more than the $600,000 needed just to pay the mortgage off. You need more than that in after-tax income. You still need to live and pay those high taxes.

It is a wonder that some employees have enough income left each month to contribute to retirement savings. It turns out that many do not. In fact, about 40 per cent of Canadians do not always have enough to meet their regular expenses. Following this model means trying to invest after you have been taxed on your income. It presents a significant problem if there is not enough left over after everyone has put their hands in your pocket and taken a share. This explains why so many people have such high levels of debt – debt for stuff, not debt that can be used to leverage an asset.

Is it that incomes are too low and not keeping pace with costs? Perhaps partially. Is it that so many people are bad at planning their cash flow? Or is there a larger problem? Is something systemically wrong with how our society works?

I believe the problem can be helped significantly by proper financial education. There is a missing link in education for a large proportion of people and I would like to ensure they receive it and use it.

Taxation is a necessary part of living in an organized and caring society, but it should not become a trap. Much of the taxation system is geared to favour large corporate entities to dissuade them from moving to other provinces, states, or countries. Yet many individuals have discovered how to make money work for them while avoiding paying excessive amounts of income tax. These are the people who are in the B and/or I quadrants on the passive income side of Kiyosaki's quadrant. Your goal should be to get yourself into these two quadrants. The tax system can be made to work more in your favour when you are an investor or a business owner. You do not have to be mega-rich like Warren Buffet, Donald Trump, or Mitt Romney to pay much less tax.

Pay Less Tax

If you want to be rich, learn to think like the rich and play the game their way. Become educated about financial matters, because when you live most of your life in the B and I quadrants, you will know how to keep more of your wealth and put it to good use. The poor and middle class work for their money. Being wealthy means putting your money to work for you.

If you are currently on the left side of Kiyosaki's cash flow quadrant, there are few tax deductions for you: charitable donations, contributing to retirement savings, occasional work-related expenses, and, in the United States, writing off a portion of the interest from the mortgage. Those on the right side can take advantage of many tax breaks, on top of the fact that they don't earn their money by trading for time and energy like an employee. They legally avoid many taxes by generating passive cash flow through investments and business ownership. Some of these people in the B and I quadrants also create jobs for others by doing this.

Later, I will discuss investing in mortgages and leveraging equity to your advantage. Owning more than one piece of real estate is a great way to generate income and reduce tax, especially if you rent property to others.

This chapter is about cash flow, the operative word being 'flow'. Therefore, keep your money from, and for, your investments *moving*. Try not to let it become static. Cash flow is very important for your wealth and for your taxation strategy. Keeping money parked in mutual funds, bonds, equities, cash, or gold does not put it to work effectively. I know many financial advisors recommend these investments, but it is better to have investments that generate revenue that gets paid to you regularly. Take that cash flow and reinvest it. If you let it sit still, it is more likely to be taxed. A good financial advisor and strategist, or simply a good accountant, will show you where and how you may be able to reduce or avoid taxation.

Even if you keep money moving by selling your real estate, there are ways to offset or defer things like capital gains tax. This is just one area where the wealthy can continue to generate high earnings with lower income tax rates than the average person.

You can do the same. It requires learning and, yes, it requires a courageous shift in thinking and outlook. But would you prefer to continue working the old-fashioned way for your money and paying higher taxes? Would you be content to follow the traditional pathway of squirrelling away some savings into a retirement account and hoping that your pension will fill the gap or that your eventual house sale will provide a large enough nest egg for you? Your accountant can give you the details on how to make this happen. If you don't have an accountant, you can find one on my power team, which you will find access to at the back of this book.

From my perspective, passive income is much better than employment income. Passive income is earned from cash-flowing assets, not from the sweat off your brow. Passive income provides far more opportunities to reduce your tax payable and to invest in more assets, all while making you less 'enslaved' as an employee.

Of course, you need to learn how. That is why you are reading this book.

* * *

5

HOW THE BANKS WORK

Yo ou don't often see big banks go bankrupt, do you? Thanks to their proven business model, banks post solid profits pretty much every year. In short, banks dominate the business world, providing what amounts to be essential services. Of course, bank failures do occur sometimes, especially as a result of financial crises like in 2008/09, but they are relatively few. For average bank customers, a failure doesn't affect them much. They continue using their cheques and cards and keep paying their mortgages that are taken over by another bank. Meanwhile, most banking institutions are backed by insurance companies that are, in turn, assured by government. So, even in the event of problems, banks remain safer and more secure than other businesses.

When it comes to financial planning, investing and success, there is much to be learned from how banks operate. Look at the downtown core in pretty much any big city and you'll see banks clustered on prominent corners of busy precincts. These are among the most expensive addresses situated on prime business real estate. Banks can afford the huge price tags for these high-profile locations because their business methods are so profitable. Clearly, their way of doing things is working.

So, what should *you* do when you see a successful business like a bank? You should find out how it does business, follow its lead, and imitate its model. As much as you may want to create your own business system, don't ignore a centuries-old method of making big profits. Copy what succeeds and recreate that model for your own success.

Please note that in a way I am lumping all banks together here for convenience. There are many kinds of banks. For the sake of you and your money, I am referring to the fundamentals of banking that work like this: people put their money in a bank for safekeeping and then the bank uses it elsewhere to create profit for itself and its shareholders.

When you boil it right down, a bank sells products and services like any business does. The main product it sells happens to be money. The services it sells revolve around storing, lending, and increasing money. Customers essentially purchase security for their money, easy access to their money, opportunities to increase their money, and opportunities to borrow more.

So, what makes the banks so spectacularly profitable? And how can you mimic some of their success? Their way of doing business can be a blueprint for your own wealth building and financial freedom.

How Banks Generate High Profits

Banking in its simplest form starts with customers placing their money in a bank. That bank then lends that money to others, who use it to buy a home or business, or buy a car, or travel, or invest, or many other purposes. This successful business practice has been around since human beings first placed value on material things.

Banks generate significant revenue by charging interest on money they lend. The borrower ends up repaying more than the original borrowed sum, essentially paying a fee for using the money-lending service.

With a home mortgage, the borrower typically pays that fee in the form of an interest rate, around three or four per cent in the second decade of the 2000s. There are other loan products available to consumers at higher rates. Then there are credit cards, for which banks charge interest rates from 18 to 28 per cent, sometimes higher, thus significantly increasing revenue even more. In addition, there are business loans.

A significant part of banking, in simplified terms, occurs when you deposit money. When you place money in a bank savings account or term deposit, the bank essentially borrows from you and uses your money to make more money for itself. The bank pays you interest for your deposit at rates it has worked out carefully. Usually those rates are low. The bank calculates and adjusts them according to interest rate policies set by the institution that governs a country's banking system. (In the United States, that is the Federal Reserve Bank. In Canada, it is the Bank of Canada.) That bank also charges interest on loans it provides. The interest rate that a bank charges on loans is always higher than the interest rate it pays on deposits it is holding. This ensures profit. Of course, the bank is duty bound to ensure that its customers' deposits are protected, yet at the same time it can even offer more credit than it has cash on hand. This is crucial. Banks use this approach to generate very high profits. So can you. More about it later in this chapter.

While the bank promises to protect the money you have saved up and deposited, the key is what it does with that money. It is not profitable to merely hold onto it. If it were, sticking money in a mattress would be as good as using a bank. Revenue is generated from investing that money, lending it out, and by leveraging up its potential value. In the current financial climate, a bank pays account holders maybe one or rarely two per cent interest on savings account balances, and a little more for term deposits. It may make significant profit lending the money out and charging interest, just as it will investing in the stock market, while paying its customer the agreed smaller interest rate. It's simple and it works. Calculate and apply the appropriate net interest margin (sometimes called 'spread') and it is a very profitable practice.

Interest Margin or Spread

Interest margin is a system calculated by a bank to take in more money from charging loan interest than it pays out in interest on customer deposits. Think, for example, of a bank that has 100,000 customers, each with $1,000 deposited. That's $100 million! If the bank pays one per cent interest on those deposits, keeps 20 per cent in reserve, and lends 80 million at an average of five per cent interest, it stands to make millions more in profits. That bank will still come out well ahead even if five or 10 per cent of those loans are written off due to customers defaulting on repayment. This partially covers the risk involved in lending money.

Risk and Reward

Yes, there is risk in lending, despite how powerful the banks appear. No bank can ever know absolutely that it will get back all the money it lends. Aside from checking a borrower's credit history, financial status, and income stability (especially employment), a bank covers risk cleverly. First, collateral covers the amount of the loan. With a mortgage, the home is used as security (collateral) against risk. If the borrower cannot repay the loan, the bank can sell the home and recoup a significant portion of its costs. For a car loan, a bank may use the car as security. Also, the bank usually takes out insurance on a mortgage loan, which the borrower pays for up front. On top of all that, for riskier loans that have less security, the bank will charge higher interest rates, so if any of these loans go bad, it is still receiving enough repayments and interest to ensure a profit in the big picture. With prudent operations, the number of loans going bad is usually very low and losses to the bank are minimal.

When a bank invests in businesses by providing them with loans, it verifies the value of businesses. It provides funds to those that are already profitable and that have assets the bank can potentially sell or even take over. These assets provide the bank with something to secure the money it lends. It is rare to see a bank lend to a business that is not making any profit.

Banks in the 21st century generate further revenue and profits through many more processes (i.e. products) than just deposits, investments and loans. They offer credit cards, consumer banking, commercial banking, retail banking, asset management, investment banking and services, financial planning services, market trading, stocks, bonds, currency trading, commodity trading, payment services (how money is transferred to a merchant when a purchase is made by credit or debit cards), global banking services, and much more.

Even greater revenue is gathered through charging fees and providing interchange services. No doubt you've experienced fees and charges yourself: account servicing fees, transaction charges, overdraft fees, mortgage fees, processing fees, ATM fees, late payment charges, card replacement fees, stop payment fees, and many more. Fees make up a good chunk of banks' revenues. Interchange is the processing of credit card and debit card transactions.

The banks charge fees for processing the transactions and hence can afford to offer reward programs for using their credit cards.

Another significant thing banks do to enhance their profits is to reduce expenses, especially by automating systems where possible. Over the years, we have seen the rise of ATMs, telephone banking, online banking, and banking mobile apps.

How Can You Emulate the Banks?

Step back a moment and look at the bigger picture and how it applies to you. When banks provide your mortgage, you pay maybe two or three per cent compounding interest on what you borrowed. When you have a credit card, you pay 18 to 28 per cent.

Meanwhile, that bank gives out no more than one or two per cent interest on savings accounts and deposits, while it is making much more for itself. On top of that, it charges fees for using its services. The bank is more than tripling its money.

Wouldn't you like to make money by using some of the techniques the banks use? Maybe you can't be a bank yourself and lend money, but there are other ways you can use the banks' know-how to enhance your wealth significantly. I'll talk more about how the banks use the power of leverage in chapter seven, 'Leveraging Equity'.

Edie and Dale

Banks also rely on their assumption that most of their clients don't read the fine print. Just ask my clients Edie and Dale.

Edie and Dale were successful professionals in their early 50s. They'd managed their money well and had several investments as well as a big home on a large piece of property north of Toronto. The promise of retirement had them looking for ways to leverage their assets to maintain their lifestyle even after they retired and their income was reduced. They were very clear that they were looking for options that did not deplete their capital, and they wanted to generate between $5000 and $7000 per month.

I encourage my clients to look around at all their investment options, and before we developed a plan Edie and Dale went to the bank. They were wowed by what the bank had to say and they came to show me the paperwork.

I took the weekend to look over what the bank had provided. I knew that my clients were looking for investment vehicles that would pay them every month without reducing their capital. I got pretty upset over the bank's documentation. I work in the financial industry, study the financial industry, and I found the documents prepared by the bank confusing.

The bank had helpfully circled what they wanted Dale and Edie to see. But when I read every tiny word it became clear that what the bank was proposing was to pay them *from their own principal*. True, they'd keep their money in investment vehicles that paid an average return of eight per cent. But the monthly payments back to my clients was coming out of their principal. I wanted to be sure, so I called up one of my lawyer buddies and asked him to review it as well. He read the same thing.

I called Dale and Edie to tell them what I interpreted, and suggested they go back to the bank to confirm. It was true. The bank was not actively investing their capital to produce income off the growth. It was simply converting their money to monthly payments, and eventually the money would run out.

So, by all means do what the banks do, but do not necessarily do all your investing with the bank. Read the fine print and get someone else to read over documentation before you sign on the dotted line.

Take Control: Make Money Work for You

Coming back to mortgages, banks ensure profitability with repayment terms that cover 25-30 years. It takes that long to pay off because the borrower pays compound interest on the money. Two, three, or four per cent interest on the surface may *seem* low, but it is not a matter of simply calculating that percentage of the amount borrowed and adding it to the total. Go online to use a free mortgage calculator and you will see that for a $400,000 mortgage at three per cent the typical amount of interest to pay over 30 years is more than $200,000. There is a lot of compounding involved in mortgage interest.

So, mortgages are very profitable. Bank employees likely won't tell you that, of course. Nor will they tell you that you will pay hundreds of thousands of dollars in interest on your mortgage (unless you ask). Furthermore, many may not tell you the simple methods of paying off that mortgage faster. The longer it takes for the mortgage to be paid off, the more money the bank makes. Furthermore, many banks offer mortgages that require you to pay off much more interest early in the term before your payments start to reduce the principal sum you borrowed. The bank wouldn't make much revenue if your payments reduced both interest and principal at the same time.

Fortunately, help is at hand. You can take back control over your finances.

There is a proven system at davidpayoffmymortgage.com that has helped over 30,000 clients. By revealing the secrets of the banks and how they operate, this system has shown people how to get around much of that compound interest and how to put a lot of money towards just their mortgage principal and pay it off as fast as possible. This is important because paying off your mortgage faster reduces your costs, reduces your debt load, and opens up more equity in your home for you to invest in other things.

Banks know that you are richer than you think. By owning a home and maximizing it properly, that home could make you a multi-millionaire. You can take control of your financial future instead of leaving it to others. Unfortunately, not enough people are tapping into their resources because they simply don't know how. They carry on taking their money and investing it in mutual funds, or leaving it in a bank savings account to earn one to two per cent, or they are investing in their RRSPs and 401(k)s.

That's all just paper. By that I mean something that essentially has no *real* value. The money may be invested, but people are not entirely certain what the fund is investing in. The fund may provide a description, but it is essentially allowed to dictate the terms and remove control from the investor. If the fund loses 30 per cent, the client must simply accept it and there is almost no way to check if what the fund managers say about it is right. Maybe the fund performance did indeed drop, but how do you check if it actually lost as much as you did? Or if it gained in value, how do you check that the fund passed on the full benefit?

The solution is always to take more control over your investments and diversify. Don't leave your money in a bank account that pays a measly one to two per cent when the bank is making a lot more money from it. That bank also charges fees for every time you access, withdraw, or use your own money. Just consider that carefully for a moment: you are paying fees to access your own money that the bank is using to make profits. To me, that's double dipping.

Now, I am not highlighting all this to say anything is wrong with the banks. I understand business and the banks are in business. They are in business for the same reason as everybody else: to make money.

Their system is working for them and has been for many, many years. It's a system that produces profits and success.

The good news is that, just like the banks have a proven model, you also have a proven model of success and wealth building available to you right now. It mimics how the banks do things and it is not as risky as some people may think, simply because it is transparently obvious how profitable that system actually is. What the banks do is really no secret.

Instead of reinventing the wheel by pursuing your own methods, our goal and your goal is to duplicate the pathway to success.

* * *

6

HOME OWNERSHIP

W hy do you need to own a home? I will just come out and say it. Renting is a waste of money. Waste. Of. Your. Money. Although the economy may need renters, it needs home owners more. Everyone has a place in this economy, but if you are looking to create your own financial independence, renting is not going to help you.

I encourage renting when you own the property and the renter is paying you every month. I discourage renting when it means you're paying someone else every month and not getting anything else out of it. Think about it for a minute and see if you can ever remember 'being wealthy' and 'being a renter' used in the same sentence. It just doesn't happen that often, unless you're making a point the way I just did. :-)

Let's Talk About Assets

Assets are resources with economic value that can provide a benefit in the future. That future benefit could be to generate cash flow or reduce expenses. For individuals, this benefit is usually cash, or something that can be converted into cash, such as securities, real estate or other property, a vehicle, receivables (money someone owes you), and, if you have a business, it would also include inventory and office equipment.

One of the common denominators of the wealthy is the accumulation of assets. Your home is an asset that has the capacity to generate income for you independently. Your car is an asset but only insofar as the cash you can generate from selling it, factoring in depreciation. The minute you buy your car it begins depreciating and continues to be worth less and less over its lifetime. Your home does the opposite. Your home is in the class of assets that are wealth builders. It has the capacity to generate wealth for you without you having to do much at all. Let me give you an example.

Let's talk about purchasing a $400,000 property. You'll need to put five per cent down to purchase it.

$400,000 x .05 = $20,000.

With your $20,000 down payment on your $400,000 property, you've got a mortgage of $380,000.

Your property appreciates at an average of five per cent in the first year. (This is not at all out of the realm of possibility, with growth rates in Toronto and Vancouver frequently in double digits. In fact, in December 2016 alone, Toronto house prices increased a whopping 19.7 per cent.) At just five per cent appreciation, that $400,000 property gained $20,000 in value in the first year you've owned it, and you've done nothing except make the mortgage payments. Suddenly, you have a home worth $420,000, which is $40,000 more than the mortgage you started with. In other words, you just doubled the $20,000 you put down.

Let's take a look at that same $20,000 when you're a renter. You take that $20,000 and put it in the bank. Perhaps you have an outstanding arrangement with your bank and you get a one per cent interest rate on your $20,000.

$20,000 x .01 = $200. Big whoopy. And the bank will look at you as a renter with $20,000 in the bank, and peg your net worth at... $20,000.

Back to the $400,000 home purchased with the $20,000. For the sake of this demonstration, let's just say your mortgage didn't change and it stayed at $380,000. Your net worth is now the value of the property ($420,000), less the liability of your $380,000 mortgage. Your net worth is $40,000. Again: doubled in just one year! Your net worth is also double that of the renter who did the 'responsible' thing and put the $20,000 into an interest-bearing savings account. In the latter scenario, the bank is thanking you. But are you thanking you?

Imagine this process over five years. You continue to incrementally pay your mortgage down from $380K to $360K and then to $340K. Meantime your house appreciates from $400K to $420K to $440K and then $460K! You are widening the gap between your former renter self and your home owner self and you are considerably boosting your net worth. You haven't really had to do anything to make that happen, except buy the house in the first place. You can just sit there and have your house make you money every single year. When you are a renter you cannot do that. You're stuck as a renter.

This is why it's absolutely necessary to get into a home. You want to make your money work harder than you do. Getting into a home as an owner is a golden nugget game-changer. Once you get into the home, you start to build equity. And equity is the thing that will change your life forever. So, how do you get the financing to help you become a home owner?

Most people will answer that question by pointing to the big banks. True, the banks will usually lend you up to 80 per cent of the value of the home, or 95 per cent if it is insured. Private lenders may sometimes go as high as 90 per cent. The interest rates will differ because the level of risk is different. But, in either case, banks or private lenders will enter into the loan agreement because they keep the home as security. It's called a lien, and it means that until you've satisfied the terms of the agreement, if anything should go wrong with your ability to pay, the lender gets the first option to sell the property and recoup some or all of their funds.

But you still need to have that first five to 20 per cent for the down payment, right? How do you get that? Sorry, no tricks for this one. Save, save, save. And then save some more. You can borrow from your RRSPs to generate a down payment, or, if you're in the United States, borrow from your 401(k). You can ask your parents to borrow from their equity. You can let the tax man fund your down payment by using and saving your income tax refunds. Whatever it takes to get into a house. It's a necessity and it's mandatory for creating financial independence.

So, let's talk about the mortgage. What is it that the lenders look for? They look for three things: credit score, income, and down payment.

Aish and Anjali

Aish and Anjali were referred to me by a real estate agent. They were ready to take the plunge and buy their first home. Aish has an engineering background and had lots of detailed questions. He'd done his research online before our first appointment and the young couple walked in ready to take the lead in our conversation. Aish perched at the front of his chair, leaning into the desk with his elbows on his knees. His wide-open eyes behind rimless spectacles gave his tension away. Even though he'd read everything he could about buying a home and getting a mortgage, he was a little overwhelmed. Anjali sat back, looking from me to her fiancee and back as we went through the details. I knew they just wanted everything to be all right. We took it slowly, determined the price range they could afford in a home, and I got them pre-approved for their first mortgage.

Aish and Anjali were like any other first-time homebuyers, in terms of the process to get them a pre-approved mortgage so they could start looking at homes with confidence. Aish's income was good and together with Anjali's they were going to be able to qualify for a mortgage to get them a great starter home.

Qualifying for a Mortgage

Every lender needs essentially the same types of information in order to assess an application for credit, even when your home is going to secure the debt.

Income

If you're an employee, you will need to produce a job letter along with two recent pay stubs. You can expect your HR department to receive a call from the lender, sometimes two. I will often call the HR department before the lender calls just to ensure it's ready with the right information. When a lender contacts an employer while assessing a mortgage application, questions will often be about the hourly rate or salary, any bonuses, what the job title is, and sometimes even the job description.

If you're self-employed, you will need to produce the three most recent notice of assessment documents from the Canada Revenue Agency. Three years are required because the self-employed often have much greater fluctuation in personal income year over year and the lender will look for a trend. The lender will also look for a website presence and company phone number, and sometimes they will ask for invoices you've issued and even bills that you've paid.

Credit Score

You will need to sign a permission waiver giving the lender the right to access and check your credit score. We already went through this in chapter three, 'Credit and Credit Score', so you know how it works. You'll want to be sure your credit score is above 650, or it will be difficult to get a lender interested in your file, no matter how high your income or your down payment.

Down payment

You will need to provide more than just the amount of your down payment. Money laundering rules in Canada mean that the lender needs to know exactly where your money is coming from and we will need to see at least 90 days' worth of bank statements. So, if you have a total of $40,000 available for a down payment, but it is split between three banks and a credit union, you will need three months of statements for each account in each institution you will access to provide the down payment. If the down payment was a gift, you will need adequate proof of that.

Changing Mortgage Rules

The Canadian government has made numerous rule changes regarding mortgage lending since the market crash of 2008. The changes have been mainly to protect consumers by making it more difficult to enter into higher-risk mortgages. A higher-risk mortgage is one with anything less than 20 per cent down. Here are the rules for federally regulated mortgage lenders as of this writing.

- The maximum amortization period for a mortgage is usually 25 years. At one point, it was 40 years, but government regulators feared this was allowing people to get into a home and a mortgage when they really couldn't afford it. The risk of default, losing the home, and even bankruptcy was too high.
- Banks must use as a benchmark the Bank of Canada's posted interest rate for a five-year fixed mortgage. This is a higher rate than most borrowers will be paying, but it has brought a little more conservative lens to the mortgage lending world.
- The maximum total debt service (TDS) ratio is 44 per cent and the maximum gross debt service (GDS) ratio is 39 per cent. These ratios are important measures of your ability to pay back debt. The TDS is the share of your total income required to service all your debt, including credit cards and car loans, as well as your household expenses. The GDS is how much of your total (gross) household income goes toward expenses related to your home, including heating, property taxes, and mortgage payments.
- The minimum down payment required to get into a mortgage and buy a home or condo is five per cent. For homes between $500,000 and $999,999, an additional 10 per cent of the amount of the home over $500,000 must be added to the down payment.

Interest Rates

Aish had read all about interest rates and was eager to get a mortgage with the lowest possible interest rate. On the face of it, a wise desire.

Less interest means less money paid out over the term of the mortgage, right?

Not necessarily.

Aish had done his online research and already had a number in his head: nice and low, and he was calculating what his mortgage payments would be at that rate. I had to explain that the mortgage with the lowest interest rate may not necessarily be the best mortgage for his circumstances.

Often, low interest rate mortgages are more restrictive. If you want to pay off a big chunk with that nice bonus from work, or you want to sell your home for any reason within the term, your penalties are going to be three times higher. So, you can't just look at the rate.

Fixed Vs. Variable

Your interest rate will be driven largely by whether you choose a fixed-rate or variable-rate mortgage. Both will provide you with the financing you need to buy your home, but they are quite different.

With a fixed-rate mortgage, you will know exactly what interest rate you'll be paying through the full term of your mortgage (your term can be anywhere from six months to five years), so there is certainty around what your payments will be, how much interest versus principal you are paying off within your term, and cash flow planning is simpler. The fixed rate mortgage is for those who tend to be more risk averse. With a fixed-rate mortgage, you pay a little more for the security of knowing your rate, and typically the fees for breaking the contract (selling the home or paying it down early) can be high.

A variable-rate mortgage, on the other hand, means your interest rate will fluctuate with the market over your term. If rates go down, you benefit. If rates go up, you pay the higher rate. It takes a little more flexibility when planning your cash flow, but the statistics show that over the long term the variable-rate mortgage will save you money. And if you want to pay the mortgage down early, or pay it off altogether, often the fees for breaking the contract are as low as three months' interest.

So, with Aish, I recommended a mortgage that would give him the flexibility to use his annual bonuses from work to pay down his mortgage faster without penalty. In fact, he could make a 20 per cent pre-payment every year without incurring costly penalties. I showed him how this would save him more than a few percentage points compared with the lowest possible interest rate mortgage that came with all kinds of restrictions. Once he saw the numbers, he was satisfied.

Completing the Mortgage Application

Precision is important when filling out a mortgage application. While a nurse and personal support worker might sound very similar, you will get yourself into trouble if you put one title on the mortgage application and another on the forms you fill out with your lawyer. Don't tell me, as your mortgage broker, that you're an electrical engineer and then tell your lawyer you're an electrical technology specialist. Everything must match.

Offering and Buying

Just because you are pre-approved does not mean you have your mortgage fully approved. That means any offer you and your real estate agent decide to enter into should still include a condition on financing.

Once you find a home and put in an offer that is accepted, it is time to plan for closing. I advise you to take the closing or possession day off work. You can expect to have multiple appointments to finalize signatures and pick up keys. But don't plan to do anything else that day because anything can still happen. Whatever you do, don't plan to move into your new house the day you get your keys! That's a recipe for disaster. There are often unforeseen delays, and you don't want to add to the stress by having a fully-loaded moving truck with nowhere to go.

Timing of Other Purchases

Aish and Anjali were getting married, and buying that first three-bedroom semi-detached home was just one of many life changes they were heading into. When we were filling out the original mortgage pre-approval application, Aish asked my advice about how much they should spend on the new car they were going to need once they had their home. I'm so glad he asked me first!

My advice to him was to let the mortgage application and home purchase process go through before buying a car. Particularly because they were planning to finance the vehicle, I told him that the extra hits on his credit file may cause some difficulties with the mortgage approval process. I suggested they wait until after closing to get the car. It's easier to get a car loan with a mortgage already in place than it is to get a mortgage application approved while you're obviously shopping for more credit.

Consider Property Taxes and Bills

It's easy to get all worked up about squeezing every penny possible out of a mortgage to get the most house you can afford. That's especially common in the Canadian markets of Toronto and Vancouver, with double-digit property price growth and multiple bidding wars. But the danger with that is finding yourself in your new home, unable to afford to pay property taxes, heat and hot water and electricity bills.

Do your research up front. Know what the taxes and utility costs will be before you put in your offer. If you let yourself get squeezed right at the beginning, you will not have enough left over to live, let alone pay down your mortgage to leverage the investment and create financial freedom.

Rent to Own

There is another option for becoming a home owner. It's a bit unorthodox, but I've made it work hundreds of times. It's rent to own. My rent-to-own program is a win-win for both investors and the new home owners. From the investors' perspective, it is a different sort of real estate investment. You're still buying property and gaining passive income from it, but you're helping people that otherwise wouldn't be able to get into and own a home.

Ursula

When I met Ursula, she had just fled an abusive relationship in Winnipeg and was trying to start anew in Toronto. She had some money that she could put toward a down payment, but not enough. And her credit score – because she'd been living under the shadow of an abusive partner who wouldn't allow her to put anything in her name, therefore denying her a credit history – was virtually non-existent. So getting a mortgage in her own name was not possible.

I pulled together investors that agreed to work with Ursula in my rent-to-own program. She got to look for and choose the house. I had an investor put his name on the property, but Ursula lived there and paid the mortgage. She took care of all the maintenance on the property – everything was as though the home was 100 per cent hers.

Which it was, just with the help of investors in a rent-to-own arrangement.

After just three years, Ursula had stabilized her employment, increased her income and established a solid credit score. In those three years, we transitioned the investors out and Ursula got the mortgage in her name. Now she's completely in control of her home, and she's working to save up money to invest in another rent-to-own scenario to help someone else. And guess what that will do? That will put Ursula on the path to financial independence.

My Rent-to-Own Program

I do it backwards from the way most people expect. I find the tenant first. It takes the right kind of person for my rent-to-own program to work. The candidates I find likely have a credit issue like Ursula, often because they're newcomers to Canada and simply haven't been able to create a credit record. They need some sort of down payment, both to have skin in the game and to show our investors they are serious. These are good people with bad or no credit who deserve a break.

Next, I pair them with an investor who agrees to fund the remainder of the down payment and carry the mortgage. Because we want this to be as close to the first-time home-buying experience as possible, we don't purchase the home in advance. That would risk forcing a new buyer into a home they may not love. So, we look at their situation, and determine the price range that they qualify for in a new home. It may be $200,000, $300,000 or $400,000. Then they go house shopping.

They choose the home that they want, in the same way they would in any other first-time home buying experience. I find that this means they have a stronger connection to the house and they really own the process. They take better care of the maintenance because it is theirs. And then, depending on how long it takes to repair their credit, we exit them out of the deal and turn the property fully over to them.

How the Payments Work

Ursula probably paid between $200 and $500 dollars more per month than the mortgage was on her home. But what that represented was the down payment for when she completely took over the mortgage from the investor and the risk the investor was taking for her.

Here's how we set the payments on our rent-to-own projects.

When you purchase a house for $300,000 today, we know the house will be worth maybe $315,000, $320,000 or $325,000 in three years. We agree on a standard appreciation and, in the contract we sign with the rent-to-own client, we use this to set an exit price based on whether you buy the house outright in one year, two years, or three years.

So, now the investor has provided the down payment and has to pay a monthly mortgage of $2,000. Of course, the investor must have all his expenses covered, so he'll charge an extra amount over and above the actual mortgage payment. This is set with what works for the client's budget and to give them a little extra cash flow every month. Yes, the investor is doing this to help the client, but also to generate positive cash flow. So, the investor makes a little extra cash every month and has a contract with the client that guarantees the increase in equity from buying at $300,000 and selling the property back to the client in two to five years at $320,000 or $330,000.

Part of the money over and above what's needed for the mortgage payment that the client pays every month is what we call an option. If the client contributed five per cent of the down payment for the $300,000 home, the down payment amount will grow as the value of the home grows, because five per cent of $300,000 ($15,000) is not the same as five per cent of $320,000 ($16,000). So, part of that option money is making sure there is enough in the kitty to cover the down payment and all other closing costs when it comes time for the renter to take over the property and the mortgage.

This program works so well because both cash and compassion motivate the investor to see the client succeed. Yes, there could be excellent cash flow for the first few years. But to fully recover the principal and to benefit from the price growth, the client must succeed as well.

And because this is actually the client's house, the client takes complete care of it and all routine maintenance. The investor is not the landlord. If there's something really big required, like a new roof, then we work out a plan where the investor can help and we deal with the financial offset in a way that works for both parties.

This rent-to-own program is not a widely known option for getting into a home as an owner. But it's very cool and rewarding to go through the process. The new home owners are very thankful, because without it they were looking at years and years before they could get into a home, if at all. They didn't know there was any help for them.

They find this opportunity by taking a leap of faith. It might be by responding to one of my ads. It could be through an open and transparent conversation with someone where they reveal their vulnerability. It could be that someone says to them, "Hey, I know somebody who might be able to help you. Why don't you give David Rhodd a call?" By letting themselves be vulnerable, they opened the door to an opportunity that could 'change their stars'.

How can this work? Is it legal? I get asked these questions all the time. Yes, it's legal. Everything is above board and it is a fantastic way to help those who might not otherwise be able to own a home. It is also a way to help investors who are looking for a new alternative investment opportunity.

Every home owner can become an investor. Using the equity acquired from a first home, or multiple properties, allows individuals to purchase more real estate and sell for a profit, or rent them out and receive monthly revenue. The key is taking that money out and putting it in a predictable and secure profit-producing investment that yields a higher return than what is being paid on the borrowed funds. It's all about leveraging equity.

* * *

7

LEVERAGING EQUITY

I am so glad I did not follow the advice of my financial advisor. Wait. What?

Okay, there is a back story and a proviso here. I am not telling *you* to ignore financial advice – unless the advisor seems to ignore your request or doesn't understand what you are talking about, which is what once happened to me.

It was some years ago, before I was in the financial industry myself. I had purchased a home as my principal residence. Then, as is typical for me, I was curious to learn more, this time about property investment. I read the book called *Is Your Mortgage Tax Deductible? – The Smith Manoeuvre* by Fraser Smith, a Canadian financial strategist. The principles of this book advocate taking the equity from your home or obtaining another kind of loan and investing the money into real estate, stocks, mutual funds, and so forth. When you borrow to invest like this, the interest you are charged on the loan can be a tax deduction against income you receive from the investment, sometimes even generating a tax refund instead of a bill. When you make a return on the investment, you can take that money and do whatever you want with it.

So, I told my financial advisor that I had read the book and wanted to try its approach. I asked him what he thought. After all, it was supposed to be his area of expertise. I remember his answer very clearly: "Don't do it. It's too risky."

But, for some reason, I remained curious. I went back to him and asked more about *Is Your Mortgage Tax Deductible? – The Smith Manoeuvre*'s ideas and why he thought they were so risky. It turned out he knew nothing about it. He had not even read the book and was not up to speed on the latest developments of using equity to invest.

I remember being stunned. This person was supposed to be guiding me by providing thorough knowledge. Here I was researching, reading, and trying to figure out how to do things that could make my life better. But when I first brought ideas from my research to an expert in the field, he could not even bother to be honest and say that he had no knowledge of these concepts. He didn't even offer to find out more. He said confidently that I should not pursue investing through mortgage equity because it was risky. He had no validation for his view whatsoever other than his position of authority.

I found a new financial advisor immediately.

Then I went ahead and did it. I followed the book, took the equity I had paid into my house, put it into a line of credit, and invested in more condos. I had to wait a couple of years to see a return because the real estate market went down for a while. Nonetheless, from what I recall, from the $60,000 I invested, my profit was $70,000. That's right, I got my principal back plus another $70,000. When I took the principal and profit out of the investment, I was able to pay it all into my mortgage and bring its balance down significantly. Looking back, if I had followed my advisor and done nothing, I would not be where I am in my life now.

In finance, the transfer of property – like with a mortgage – is called an assignment. They're common with new-build condos, where early investors buy up units before the builder has finished the project. When those investors want to sell or transfer the property rights of that unit, also before the condo development is complete, it's called an assignment.

At the time, around 2008 to 2010, that condo assignment was only my first of several investments. I went through turmoil with all my other investments to the point that the condo deal became my only one. Before then, my other investments had been performing very well and generating excellent profits. I actually wanted to cash out my property investment, but because it was a condo assignment I couldn't get the money out and had to leave it alone. That can be a drawback with assignments sometimes; the money is not liquid. However, it turned out to be a blessing in disguise because all the other money disappeared and my old faithful was the real estate.

I did end up acquiring some more assignments with a few business partners, but then I changed the model of my approach. Here's why.

The main drawback with any assignment can be that, after you put your money in, you do not directly receive anything from it until you reclaim that asset (or cash it out). If the market stalls or crashes, which it did with my first ones, you cannot get your money out and the property is not marketable. Meanwhile, if the area is saturated – if, for example, there are a lot of condos on the market, as is the case now – your asset does not stand out. In this instance, buyers and investors may be more likely to buy directly from condo builders, despite the risks of doing so, for a couple of reasons. First, the construction firm may be seen as more reputable and thus safer to buy from than from someone else. Second, if there is a surplus of properties for sale, the construction firm has the wiggle room to undercut and sell an asset for much less than you can if you are trying to make a profit. Meanwhile, if you decide to keep the asset and carry it all the way to the end of the assignment term before cashing it out, you must come up with even more money for mortgage closing costs and other expenses.

Home Equity

Equity is sometimes misunderstood, so my goal is to provide you with a greater understanding of how you can use the equity you have in your home.

In chapter six, 'Home Ownership', we covered the difference between renting and being a home owner. The major distinction is that ownership provides an asset to your name. This is important because that asset will appreciate year after year, depending on the state of the economy, without additional effort from you. For example, as we discussed, a property worth $400,000 has the potential to increase in value five per cent per year ($20,000).

Let's reach into the future and imagine you have five properties, all mortgage free. Each is valued at $400,000 and appreciating at five percent per year. Each property has tenants that pay you $2,000 per month. Each property is therefore generating $24,000 for you each year. Multiplying that by five means more than $120,000 in annual revenue to you.

Do you think $120,000 a year would allow you to leave your job? Would that amount of income assist in paying your bills? Would it allow you to take that vacation you have long wanted? To achieve any of those things, first you must have one property and then use it to generate residual income for you.

You may ask how you acquire four properties. The answer is to use leverage. After purchasing your first property, you pay down the mortgage balance as best you can. Reducing the balance owing builds your equity.

Very simply, equity is how much financial stake you have in a property, or how much money you have paid towards partial or complete ownership. If you pay off a $400,000 mortgage on a house, you have $400,000 worth of equity that you can leverage to improve that house or invest elsewhere. Similarly, if you pay off $200,000, you have $200,000 of equity that you can use. Essentially, you re-borrow money that you have already paid back. After all, the bank trusted you with the original amount. A bank should let you use that equity money because it can use your home as security.

At this point, some people will ask, "But isn't the idea to pay down my mortgage as quickly as possible? Wouldn't borrowing again make that slower?"

The goal is indeed to pay down your mortgage as fast as possible. A mortgage is expensive. The current average mortgage payment across Canada's major cities is around $1,750 to $1,800 per month. In markets like Toronto and Vancouver, they're much higher than that. Paying a mortgage back quicker will save you interest. So, imagine you carried a $400,000 mortgage and a monthly repayment of $1,800 for 20-plus years, but that repayment was associated with a $400,000 mortgage divided across multiple properties that you control (e.g. rent out). The cash flow from those properties would be significantly more than the $1,800 payment you're making to the mortgage each month.

The equity you gain has more power than you first realize.

Using Your Equity

I agree wholeheartedly that paying bills on time and getting out of debt are important. Just know that while you are in the process of doing that, there are models you can follow to enrich your life and your finances.

Most home owners want to pay off their mortgages as soon as possible to remove the pressure of bi-weekly/monthly payments and free up their finances. But most also have no intention of using the equity they accumulate. They see a mortgage as a very large debt with hefty amounts of interest attached that must be repaid urgently. Although that may be true, they are missing a huge opportunity. Being a home owner is but one step on an investment journey, the means to an end and not the end itself.

Don't merely pay off your mortgage and leave the equity sitting there, idle and impotent. See the bigger picture. The key is to know how to leverage that equity to your advantage. Leveraging is what the banks do to make more money. Learn from their example and use it. They have mastered a model of how to double and triple funds in reasonable amounts of time. They take equity from mortgages, deposits, and savings accounts (for example, up to 80 per cent of deposits), leave a small portion remaining in there (especially money deposited by their shareholders), and distribute the rest to secure investments that can provide profits (to the shareholders).

As you make mortgage repayments, you build up equity in your home. For example, if you have a $500,000 mortgage and have paid back $300,000, that $300,000 is your equity. You don't have to let it sit there. It is a valuable asset. It can be leveraged and put to great use, just like a bank puts its deposits to use.

Most bank mortgages will let you take a portion of your equity and invest it. For example, if you withdraw $40,000 out of your equity, you can use that as a 10 per cent deposit on the purchase of another property that's selling for $400,000. This way you will control two properties and, when they appreciate, you have the option to sell or even invest in a third property. As you build equity in multiple properties, you provide yourself with the leverage to do more and more. You are on your way to greater financial freedom.

With mortgages, banks make money from both debt and real estate. Lending out money for these loans is an investment in debt. You can do it, too. Just as a bank will lend you a few hundred thousand dollars to purchase real estate, it is also open to you investing some of that money in other mortgages.

Now, why would that bank feel like its money is secure? Because you have paid a deposit and made repayments regularly (i.e. you have provided a solid investment), while the bank has verified both the value of the property (to recoup funds should the loan go bad) and your ability to repay.

You have leveraged your money and your stake in a mortgage to increase your wealth. The risk is more yours than the bank's, but you are likely betting on properties increasing in value to the point that you can sell them and make a good profit after paying off the mortgage balances. If you were to default on repaying, the bank can sell either property. You would lose your money, or a portion of it, while the bank would recoup the loaned amount through the sale and through mortgage insurance.

So, I am showing you that, like the banks, you can invest successfully in debt, real estate, even businesses. Doing this essentially mimics their successful profit-making system.

The Trouble with the Conventional Approach

I'm sure you've heard about one of the most common approaches to paying your mortgage off sooner: switching from monthly to bi-weekly or even weekly payments. Depending on the structure, this could take as much as five years off your mortgage.

Sounds fantastic, right? Hardly any additional effort for a big result. But, when you remember that most of the mortgages today are front-loaded with interest, you're not actually saving much money.

Let's take a typical $400,000 mortgage, where you're paying $2,000 each month. For the first five years, about 75 per cent of your payment will go toward interest, and the remaining 25 per cent toward principal. The banks will still recover their costs and earn revenue from your payments.

Now let's talk about your bank accounts. If you're like most people, you have a chequing and a savings account, maybe also a line of credit. You won't be making much, if anything, by way of interest in the funds on your accounts. Maybe you'll get one per cent per year on deposits in your savings account. Not much.

Let's say your employer pays you $5,000 every month in salary. Normally you would deposit your pay into your chequing account and use the money to buy groceries, pay your hydro bill, put gas in your car, and go see a movie. Out of that chequing account, you also pay your monthly $2,000 mortgage (of which 75 per cent goes to pay interest).

At the end of the month, maybe you have $1,000 left over. Great! You transfer that into the savings account that earns one per cent interest. But when you do this, you are not putting your dollar to its best use. Let me explain.

The David Rhodd Mortgage Payoff Plan

Instead of keeping a mortgage that is front-loaded with most of the interest paid in the first five-year term of your mortgage, I recommend getting a home equity line of credit (LOC).

The way LOCs are structured is with simple interest. The bank charges you interest on the balance of your LOC today. Here's how it works.

The lender will charge you interest based on your *daily balance*. So, consider your monthly income of $5,000. When you receive it, you immediately deposit that $5,000 - all of it - into your $400,000 home equity LOC. That means your mortgage balance just went to $395,000 from $400,000. So, you'll be charged interest for that month on $5,000 less than the previous month.

But wait! Now how do you buy food and pay the bills and see that movie? Great question. I get asked this all the time. It's easy. You use your credit card. Credit cards are wonderful tools if you use them correctly. Use your credit card for 28, 29, or 30 days. You don't touch your paycheque, only your credit card. Based on the above scenario, you will have charged about $2,000 on your card by the end of that month. Now, before the credit card company can charge you interest, you pay the credit card balance from your LOC. In fact, many types of LOCs can be set up to automatically pay your credit card balance monthly, so you don't have to worry about it.

Now your line of credit balance will be $397,000 instead of $395,000. But the interest for the month will be charged on the $395,000, and going into the next month you're paying 3.2 per cent interest (for example) on $397,000 instead of earning one per cent on $2,000.

Let's look at those interest numbers.

Interest rate	Balance	Interest Owing (/year)	Interest Earned (/year)	Interest Saved (/month)	Interest Earned (/month)
3.2%	$400,000	$12,800		n/a	
3.2%	$395,000	$12,640		$160	
3.2%	$397,000	$12,704		$96	
1%	$2,000		$20.00	n/a	$1.67

By implementing this strategy, you're saving $160 that first month alone. You're saving $64 in interest with a $397,000 balance instead of $400,000, which is still $94.33 better than putting $2,000 in your savings account.

You would continue this same process every month. Each time you get paid, you dump your entire paycheque onto your LOC, use the credit card for expenses, and whatever is left over stays in the LOC. I have a program that shows you exactly how to manage this situation, because I know it can be confusing. But by following this plan, I have helped thousands of people just like you shave years off their otherwise traditional mortgage. I have seen it bring a 25-year mortgage down to between 10 and 15 years.

And, because your LOC remains accessible, you build equity faster, creating more room to leverage that equity into wealth-building and revenue-generating real estate investments.

As you pay your mortgage, take a portion of your unused equity and invest it in secure investments that provide predictable, safe, secure, and profitable returns. Easier said than done? No! Once you are prepared with the right tools and the right power team behind you, you will see the possibilities.

You can find more information about how to pay off your mortgage faster without putting more money into your bank's pocket can be found at Davidpayoffmymortgage.com.

Edie and Dale

Remember Edie and Dale from chapter five, 'How the Banks Work'? After their experience with the bank, Edie and Dale decided to work with me to leverage the equity in their home and invest in other income-producing properties.

When I first met Edie and Dale, I noted that they possessed a quiet, confident, conservatism. Dale was bald, while Edie wore her black hair short with reading glasses dangling about her chest like a necklace. Their clothes and their manner were low key, but this was a couple who knew who they were, what they were about, and, most importantly, what they wanted.

They told me they were planning to retire in the next few years and they were interested in pumping up their retirement fund as quickly as possible. They wanted to be aggressive, but still safe and secure. They understood the need to take certain risks, but they wanted to be smart about it. In addition to protecting their lifestyle through retirement, they also wanted to be sure they were going to be free to travel and leave an inheritance to their three grown children.

They had worked hard, raised their kids, done all the right things, and now they wanted to take it to the next level. They owned their home with a mortgage that had about five years left before it was fully repaid. They had some mutual funds, and they each had an RRSP they'd been contributing to for 20 years.

We employed a multi-pronged approach. First, we used equity in their home – a big, sprawling home on a large piece of property north of Toronto – to get them into two rental properties. Once they had good tenants installed and were receiving monthly income, we looked at their RRSP's.

RRSPs are sacred to many people, especially when they're approaching retirement. But Dale and Edie were open, and their RRSPs were not performing that well. We moved some of their RRSP funds into self-directed accounts that allowed them to transfer their RRSP funds from one investment vehicle to another, including property and mortgages. There are *no tax consequences or penalties whatsoever* for doing this. (Visit davidrhodd.com/selfdirected for a handy list of the institutions that accommodate these self-directed funds.)

It was going well. Soon we had Edie and Dale and a group of other investors pitching in to a $6 million condo project. That $6 million came from those self-directed RRSPs, mutual funds, and cash.

I like real estate and mortgage projects because you can see what's happening. When you invest in mutual funds, all you ever see is paper. But you can drive by this condo project every day. Dale and Edie watched the construction develop, then watched as individual owners moved in and life bloomed around it. It is a solid, real investment. You can touch it and see it. It's more than a piece of paper.

When you invest in real estate, it is asset backed: Dale's name is actually on that condo property. Every single investor in our group is listed on that property. If anything were to happen, there would be insurance that would pay out the first mortgage, and then the second mortgage, which was our $6 million.

I like helping my clients into projects that keep working for them, whether or not I'm here. They can sleep easy knowing their money is secure.

Dale and Edie had invested in a few different projects that were paying them between eight and 10 per cent. There were no management fees. When their RRSPs were invested in mutual funds, they were earning between two and three per cent, plus they were paying management fees.

It has worked out well for Dale and Edie. They're now fully retired, have liquidated their big home, and used the proceeds to invest in another three real estate projects. They're getting steady, healthy, monthly income from their investment portfolio which is now worth more than $1 million.

Buying with No Money Down

One of my mentors is Robert Allen, a financial expert and author of the New York Times bestselling book *Nothing Down: How to Buy Real Estate With Little or No Money Down.* He has since published several more books, including *Nothing Down for the 2000s: Dynamic New Wealth Strategies in Real Estate.* There is no arguing with how he has used his own successful model to enrich his life.

I've had the good fortune to spend some time with Robert. The experience transformed my thinking. He spoke in depth about leveraging and using one property to acquire another, then using two properties to purchase more, and so on. Most importantly, what I took away was how secure real estate investing can be. Robert reached his goals primarily through this method and is now a successful and financially free entrepreneur.

To be clear, in Canada you cannot buy a home and get a mortgage from a bank without a down payment. The idea behind Robert Allen's principle is that there are unconventional ways to come up with the required down payment. Robert Allen wants people to realize the investment potential and value of real estate, even if they may have the ability to qualify for a mortgage to start with, but may not have the 20 per cent deposit required to provide a mortgage on an investment property. He also understands that the traditional idea of needing excellent credit, strong financial history, good income, and stable employment is not always necessary for borrowing from banks.

The key is to first acquire one property. This is the starting point for future investing. But can a person buy a property without a large enough deposit, or even none at all?

Perhaps the most common way to do that is to borrow the deposit privately from family or friends. Another common approach is to collaborate with another investor who can supply the down payment.

There are other ways to purchase real estate with little or no deposit. Robert Allen explains that buyers often have talents or other assets that can be used in lieu of cash deposits. It requires creativity, such as borrowing against the cash value of a retirement savings plan or an insurance policy. Or perhaps using trade skills and services and discounts in exchange for a down payment. Or even leveraging an inheritance. Sometimes personal property can secure a down payment – a car, a boat, a collection, artwork, even musical instruments.

After acquiring one property and building some equity in it, there are more options for obtaining enough money to invest in another. Options include things like borrowing from private lending organizations (sometimes called borrowing hard money), buying as an owner-occupant, renting to buy, flipping or wholesaling, refinancing, obtaining a line of credit, even using credit cards (which is a very risky option).

The hard money approach with a private lending company can be expensive. Most loans are for one year and you need to pay off the balance when that one year term is up. This approach should be treated as a quick bridging method. It may appear less expensive in the short-term, but can be far more costly if held longer than that initial term.

Buying a property as an owner-occupant usually involves a loan where you agree to occupy the premises for at least one year. After that, you can turn it into an investment by renting it out. While not necessarily easy, it is sometimes possible to obtain an owner-occupied mortgage with a deposit of at least five percent. Your costs will be higher, likely due to mandatory mortgage insurance that has a high premium, but if you can do it, you will build equity that you can then use to purchase another property.

Some people purchase investment properties with little or no money down so they can flip them, meaning to sell them for a profit very soon after purchasing them. This requires a lot of advice, knowledge, skill, and risk tolerance. Flipping is sometimes called wholesaling. You need connections to find off-market properties (less expensive ones or those you find via word of mouth) and then the ability to sell them quickly for a profit.

Some investors who already have a mortgage may decide to refinance it after housing prices have risen. When the house is worth more, they can obtain a larger loan and use the extra proceeds to invest. Nobody needs to create more money, merely use what the bank will make available based on the property's value. It is a common approach when interest rates are low.

Finding an excellent financial advice team and learning from them will open your eyes to the many methods that can be used for buying an initial property and then investing in more. Many of these methods can be achieved without the traditional approach of saving up a deposit. Remember that this is using a principle that the banks themselves use.

The Power of Leverage

Leverage is using borrowed money to buy assets and expecting those assets to increase in value and revenue production so they become worth more than the cost of borrowing. That includes providing funds to buy a house using a mortgage (a bank counts a mortgage as its asset) and expecting that the mortgage interest revenue and the house's projected gain in value will substantially exceed the amount provided for the loan. When you take out a mortgage and put down a deposit, you use borrowed money to leverage the savings you put down. You don't have the money yourself for the entire purchase, but you buy it with borrowed money because you expect it to grow in value. It is similar for a bank that uses money it borrowed to provide the funding for your mortgage, expecting the loan and interest payments to provide a solid profit.

Let's revisit banks for a moment and look at how the banks use leverage. Often the main source of funds banks use for lending is the safe haven created by the deposits they hold. But knowing how to leverage those deposited funds is crucial. In the case of savings, let's use an example where there is $1 million accumulated across several client accounts. At any given time, not every client will need access to his/her money. That's why it is in a savings account. Anyone can still withdraw all of theirs immediately. By law, the bank must keep a minimum reserve. But the bank knows that not everyone will withdraw some or all of their money at the same time, except in a disaster. On average, these people might need access to about 20 per cent of that $1 million at any given point in time. That means there is

$800,000 sitting there doing little, even nothing. When banks look at savings accounts, they calculate all the money that is being under-utilized. The bank has 80 per cent that it can use to make more money by investing or lending it. This way the expected profit can keep the deposits topped up and protected. That bank is sitting on potentially several times that usable money and it can use the projected earnings in powerful ways.

The exact formulae banks use for leverage are not well known. Banks are very protective of their leverage secrets, although banking regulations limit them to protect depositors' funds. Not only are they able to use deposits based on what they calculate customers need on hand, they leverage them up to estimate their worth much higher. Using the example of $1 million on hand in deposits, the exact amount of leverage the bank can gain is difficult to determine, but a conservative estimate is that the bank sees it as being worth several million (after using it in loans and investments). In some cases, it could amount to as much as $10 or $15 million.

Banks can leverage loans as well. The expected revenue from those loans can be a powerful bargaining chip for expansion opportunities. When it comes to mortgages that have government-backed insurance, leverage of these assets can be very high. There is less leveraging with loans that aren't insured, like credit cards and car loans, so banks place higher interest rates on them to increase the interest margin, or spread.

The numbers on a bank's books reveal potential. Of course, leverage potential is not actual money – yet. In a way, you might conclude that the number they leverage up to is fake. It's not. There is a semantic and legal difference between fake money and money that has not yet been actualized. In the old days, people would talk about the gold standard because banks needed to have enough gold to account for every dollar on their books. That is not the case anymore. Now there is leverage and banks can boost that significantly.

There is nothing inherently wrong with this leveraging process where *expected* money is used to expand opportunities and boost value. As I said earlier, if banks are doing something and are successful at it, learn from it and follow the example. Wouldn't you love to take your $10,000 deposit in a bank account and leverage it at a ratio of 10:1 so it becomes worth $100,000?

Lose Your Fear

Fear limits potential.

As a society, we need to eliminate the fear about accessing and investing home equity. Often that fear is based on not understanding the concept, as demonstrated by my former financial advisor that I mentioned at the beginning of this chapter. Making equity investment work requires understanding the concept of borrowing a dollar to make two dollars. This is essentially how banks get ahead and how you can, too. Put your mortgage to work for your benefit and you can get to your financial end goal faster.

Using your equity is not a high-risk investment. Moving funds from one secure vehicle, which is your first property, to another (while still supported by the value of the initial property) is safe and should be profitable. Your money will always be safeguarded by the asset's value.

In recent years, Canadian home properties have appreciated by anywhere from five per cent to double digit percentages annually, according to the Canadian Real Estate Association. If you own a home of some kind, you are likely getting a decent return on your investment, even though that does not translate automatically to cash in your hand. With current mortgage rates around three per cent, if you were to take your equity, re-borrow it (i.e. withdraw it), and place it into an investment that is making anywhere from six to 20 per cent, you can see you would receive a very profitable return.

This is the flick of the switch that will change everything for your financial future.

If you do this, you will see your first mortgage's balance and your repayments become temporarily larger again, but only until you pay it down. But the example above shows that the profitable investment return can more than cover the higher repayments you will have from using your equity.

Learn to see profit potential in even small things and your financial outlook will change. Every one of us has, at some stage in our lives, borrowed a dollar from someone when we didn't have one of our own. Were we paralyzed by the thought of when and how we would be able to repay that dollar? Do not let fear stop you from borrowing extra dollars when you know there is a way to benefit. Make that money grow, and you will soon find that returning that money is easier than you thought. You will also have more left over.

Lose your fear of real estate, also. Real estate has been a cornerstone for making many people into millionaires and billionaires world-wide. Look at some of the big names of real estate: Wang Jianlin, Michael Otto, Donald Bren, or Rick Caruso, to name a few. They have built their billions on real estate. Even with the recommended safety of diverse investment portfolios these days, real estate should continue to be one of the safer long-term investments. It involves tangible assets – land and buildings – that people will always want. Big cities will likely continue growing, so land and buildings should stay in demand.

Real estate has greater long-term safety than some other options because it is not a quick investment. You don't put money in today and pull out a profit tomorrow or a week later. In 2016, which seemed like a volatile year, real estate appreciation was steady in most cities around the world.

Another reason not to fear is that the Canadian banking system is one of the most secure in the world with strict and prudent regulations. No Canadian banks were in danger of collapse during the global financial crisis of 2008/09, which was the worst crisis since the Great Depression.

Work towards having multiple assets that appreciate and create residual income. This is vital if your goal is to be financially free. Building up profitable, cash-producing assets is the secret to retiring at the age you want and creating the lifestyle you always dreamed of. Surely it makes sense that having assets make money for you while you sleep is better than putting in endless hours at work to improve your title, ranking, and salary. Banks do it and so can you. They follow a model of taking deposits and leveraging them to invest in real estate and mortgages that will make them money. Your home equity represents an opportunity to create secure, profitable investments.

It is good advice to associate with individuals who have achieved what you want to achieve. Listen to them, learn from them, and apply that learning to your life. Don't be sucked into the consensus of what the masses are doing with their money. Use your newfound understanding and refuse to let banks or anyone else take from you without there being any benefit to you in the long run.

Everyone is in business to make money. Use the gold nuggets of knowledge that have been laid out for you. Follow the pathway to leveraging your home and investing. As each property carries the expenses for you, enjoy lower taxes, and explore methods for paying your mortgage down faster by cutting out some of the compound interest from the banks. Paying higher interest will soon not be a concern when you are using one dollar to make two or more. Moving your equity to different assets that create cash flow and replace your work income will be the reason you are able to walk away from your job and live the lifestyle you have always desired.

* * *

8

SECURED INVESTING

W e've talked about the opportunity to take some equity out of your home mortgage and use it to invest elsewhere. The idea is that if you take a dollar out of your mortgage, you invest it in another vehicle that you hope will bring a return of more than a dollar. Growing your money is good, right?

Risk: Investing vs Not Investing

How do you know an investment is secure and safe? Obviously, you don't want to make a grave error by putting your equity into an investment that is not secure. If you lose that money you'll have to start from scratch and work to repay the mortgage balance all over again with a higher monthly payment. Suddenly your mortgage will take a much longer time to pay off and cost you much more. I get it.

No investment is guaranteed. But there is a big risk in *not* investing. That risk is that you stay exactly where you are, with exactly the same life you have now. No building wealth. Without investing, most people cannot achieve financial independence. Leaving your money in a bank to earn barely one or two per cent is more risky and wasteful than investing that money in something better, and yet still secure, in the hope of making a profitable return.

So, by all means, invest. But before you do, examine each opportunity thoroughly. Get help from an experienced mortgage broker. (I'm available.) Talk to others who have invested in the same or similar vehicles. Inform yourself. Remove the fear (fear limits potential, remember?) and choose secure investments.

What is a Secure Investment?

A secured investment is an asset-backed investment, where the asset is reasonably expected to grow in value or at least deliver a greater return when you sell it and cash out.

You already know I like to invest in real estate and mortgages. A residential property or commercial property, even with a mortgage, is tangible, almost guaranteed to increase in value based on historical data, and cannot go anywhere. Real estate almost always increases in value over time, meaning your money should be protected by the worth of the property. If you sell the property for a profit, you can pay off the mortgage and keep the proceeds. While real estate can fluctuate, it is not subject to the sudden changes and risks of stocks and shares where you can lose everything. A good real estate investment advisor can help you mitigate risk.

Your down payment of $20,000 to buy property is an investment you leverage with a mortgage. That $20,000 represents a portion of its value, and is, in my opinion, a wise and secure investment.

When you invest in a piece of property, the rule of 72 identifies how fast your principle will double, and how long it will take based on the interest rate of the investment.

The rule of 72 is a shortcut used to estimate how many years you need to double your money at a particular annual rate of return. To use the rule, you divide the rate, expressed as a percentage, into 72. The equation would look like this:

72 ÷ compound annual interest rate = # of years it will take to double your investment.

Let's use as an example a compound annual return of 8 per cent.

$$72 \div 8 = 9$$

At eight per cent interest, your principal will double every nine years. If you think that finding an eight per cent interest rate is difficult, you're wrong. You can find eight per cent by investing in syndicate mortgages, private mortgages, real estate, and some tax liens. Many second mortgages can achieve as high as a 15 per cent return. In some rent-to-own strategies, a 20 to 30 per cent per year return on your money is possible. With a 15 per cent return, money will roughly double every five years. Using those profits, you can continue to pay down the mortgage on your principal residence and free up some more equity, allowing you to invest again. You can take 50 per cent of your profits and use it to purchase more real estate properties, mortgage investments, syndicate mortgages, or tax liens. Following this path of repetition will create a cycle of overflow.

You will soon notice the mortgages on all your properties start to reduce, while equity builds. As your properties become profitable, you take the proceeds from those investments and deposit them on new properties to pay the mortgage down faster to release more equity available to you.

The Sad Side of the Stock Market

Real estate is completely unlike shares, stocks, mutual funds, RRSPs, and 401(k)s where you cannot see any physical trail of them going down the drain. When you invest thousands in these, you sign a disclosure with your investment advisor or bank and in return all you see are monthly or quarterly statements that (allegedly) tell you how your money is doing. You have no way of truly verifying much because a fund is divided into a complicated web of other smaller funds, larger funds, stocks, shares, and different companies.

For you to do a forensic analysis of all these companies and their profits or losses would be exhausting and frustrating, so all you can rely on is those regular paper statements. Whether they indicate you have gained five per cent or lost five per cent, you must accept what they say with no way of questioning or investigating.

In 2007, many people thought mutual funds were still the safest investments. After all, they had done well for a long time. But many people lost a lot of money in 2008 as the worst financial crisis of our lifetime occurred. A huge number of portfolios, including my own, were reduced by 50 per cent (or more). I lost half my money from a supposedly 'safe, secure, risk-free investment' that was earmarked for my retirement. Of course, real estate also lost big in 2008. But it has long since bounced back and continued appreciating.

The 2008 recession demonstrated that the unexpected can happen. A 50 per cent hit was a real wakeup call. It taught me to look for more secure investment options and to gain a better financial education. Instead of being satisfied with an average five per cent return in a 'safe' investment, less all the repeated fund management fees (try tracing where those go!), I took steps to bring my investments more under my own control.

I never want to experience that 2008 feeling again. I felt empty. I realized I had no way of knowing if the fund management company had made a mistake or been careless or was just caught up in the mayhem. I didn't know if fund managers had protected their own money instead of mine. I had so many questions. How could I know what happened and what did not happen? All I knew was that half my money got wiped away.

Eventually the market corrected. But who really controls the market? The big banks and investment corporations do. They hold all the funds. Controlling the money means controlling the market. If they wanted to, they could make markets dip. How do I know when a market crash is due to unforeseen circumstances, or when it's due to malpractice, or the banks making a profit from the market plunging? How do I know they weren't trading against me in 2008? There are so many variables in play at all times and this is the financial environment in which so many people trust their RRSPs and 401(k)s, hoping they will be available and sufficient when retirement comes around. At least Canadian banks were able to weather the financial storm better than US banks. But bank and market investments worldwide were badly affected. Furthermore, how many US bank executives went to prison for their role in the 2008 crash? A few, but none from the big banks. Top executives at the so-called 'too big to fail' banks have avoided any criminal charges, even as their banks paid tens of billions of dollars in fines to settle charges of wrongdoing leading up to the financial crisis.

If you control the money, you control the market... and more.

Taking Control Represents the Least Risk

Some people are shocked when they feel ready to retire but find they must continue to work because they realize the funds they saved won't be sufficient for their needs. They change their plans because they believe issues beyond their control keep changing – the fund market, tax laws, and so on.

The lesson for you? Be assertive. Take control of your money and look for secure investments that you can manage and monitor without paying management fees. My personal opinion is that this approach is much less risky than leaving retirement savings in the hands of banks and fund managers who will always profit from your savings, regardless of whether they make any money for you.

Don't get me wrong. It is always a good practice to diversify your portfolio to include segregated funds (a type of life insurance product), mutual funds, gold and secure investments. It is simply my belief that more funds should be earmarked for secure investments.

A secure investment is tangible and non-movable. Real estate property fits this definition. After investing, you have something to show for it that you can touch. You have the power to make decisions over that investment to enhance it, protect it, insure it, and sell it.

Can things go wrong? Of course. Are things guaranteed to go wrong? No!

You can mitigate your risk by studying the property beforehand and doing proper research about it. Furthermore, mortgage investing can provide you with more security than most other investments because it is possible for you to have control over both the property and over key aspects of the mortgage. How? By lending money yourself. Remember that controlling the money is power.

You may be aware that many people obtain first and second mortgages, but sometimes they haven't enough of a deposit to qualify at a bank, or their credit rating needs some work, and thus they borrow funds privately. If you have $20,000 of your own money available, you can lend that to someone who owns a property and wants a second mortgage. That person may need an extra $20,000 but will not break their first mortgage for fear of penalties. With proper documentation to protect your private loan agreement, you could lend that person $20,000 and, with the help of a lawyer, place a lien on the new property.

The advantages here are that your money is secure against the much higher value of the property (you have invested much less than its worth), you have legally protected your investment, and you can charge the person interest until they pay back the $20,000. Canada has not seen property values cut in half at rapid speed, even during financial crises. Therefore, you can be quite confident that if you ever had to recoup your money because the person stopped repaying you, or it became necessary to foreclose on that property, you would at least get your $20,000 investment back. Even if you are not receiving your regular cheques for the repayment and interest of your $20,000, you still can verify that your investment is OK. You can go see the property. You have a strong level of control and are not at the mercy of bankers or fund managers or the share market.

Tax Liens

Another way to take control of real estate investing is through a tax liens. (This is not yet as much of an investment option in Canada as in the United States.) A tax lien involves investing in unpaid property taxes. In many counties across the United States, if an owner or sometimes tenant of a property does not pay the necessary property taxes, that debt is never written off. Each county still needs that money for roads, services, and civic facilities. First, interest is charged to the owner and the debt mounts. If the owner still does not pay, the county may sell that debt to an investor instead of facing a budget deficit that would cause a loss of services to its citizens. The investor buys the property tax debt, essentially paying it off for the property owner. The owner now owes the investor, while the county gets the money it requires to keep services functioning. For late payment, the county will charge the property owner an interest penalty. For the sake of an example, let's say the taxes are $5,000 annually and the interest charged is eight per cent. (It varies from county to county and state to state.) The county may offer that same eight per cent to the investor, so essentially the investor puts up the $5,000 on behalf of the owner of the property and then can get an eight per cent return.

Everybody wins from this arrangement:

- The county receives the money it needs and does not have to alter its budget.
- The property owner who did not pay the taxes pays the eight per cent interest to the investor and has more time to raise and pay the $5,000.
- The investor makes a return on his/her money of eight per cent.
- The investor does not have to deal directly with the client (the property owner). The property owner still pays the $5,000 to the local authority, which in turn issues the money to the investor. That investor receives payments from the government.
- If an owner defaults and never pays the taxes, or does not pay for at least three years, some county and state laws allow the investor to take over the property through the foreclosure process.
- Not only does the investor reclaim the $5,000, he/she might even claim the property mortgage-free, just from covering the property taxes. This does not happen often, as the vast majority of owners pay their taxes. Why would an owner let go of a property worth hundreds of thousands just for a $5,000 per year property tax?

That is definitely a secured investment where you have control.

Use Margins to Your Own Advantage

When you purchase an investment using some of your own funds along with some borrowed funds, you're buying on margin. It helps you produce larger gains because you've bolstered your purchasing power with the borrowed funds. Is it possible for an individual to use net interest margins to their advantage just like the banks do? The short answer is yes, but the risks are higher, and any income generated will likely be subject to tax.

Consider, for example, taking out a secured line of credit. To get the lowest rate possible, that would mean it is secured by a property. Many people take out a line of credit as part of their mortgage agreement with a bank, essentially splitting their mortgage into two accounts. That secured line of credit's interest rate at the time of writing this might be somewhere around three per cent. Let's use that figure for this example. The regular mortgage account interest rate would be lower. Now imagine using money from that line of credit to invest in something that will yield five or six per cent. The difference between the three per cent mortgage and the six per cent yield is the net interest margin, or spread, and it would be to your advantage. Whether you refinance and increase your mortgage or borrow from your home equity LOC, the same rules apply with regards to the spread. You need quick and strong returns to ensure you can keep up with repayments without eating away your benefits.

Where should you invest that money from the line of credit so that you can make a profit? This requires talking to experts with a proven track record in helping people get out of mortgage debt faster and invest for wealth. (Like me. Visit davidrhodd.com.) Some low risk investments like bank-preferred shares may bring a margin of two or three per cent above your line of credit rate, but you would need a very large mortgage amount invested to really make monthly earnings worth your while for significant wealth building. Also, your earnings would be subject to tax and there is the risk of shares losing value. (There is never a guarantee that any kinds of shares will increase.) Bonds are 'safer' but not when you're trying to grow your money, because they may not yield a good enough interest margin, if any.

Even if your investment goes well, you would have used up a substantial portion of your borrowing capacity, if not all of it. Therefore, you would not have funds available for other investment opportunities. It can be risky to borrow in this manner to invest, but it is possible to make it work for some.

While we say it is usually good financial practice to follow a bank's methods of generating revenue and wealth, remember that the bank does it mostly with other people's money, not so much with its own.

Being a Lender

Another thing you can do is borrow from a bank to set up your own private lending for others, like the bank would do. You could make a profit by calculating the interest margin so the interest rate you charge others is higher than that charged by the bank when it lends to you. For example, use equity from your mortgage at its low rate of around three per cent and provide loans for cars at a rate of seven or eight per cent. Pool money together and you could lend it out yourself against property and put a lien on the title to protect your investment. Of course, you may not want to risk lending out as much as $500,000, for example. You could lend as little as $20,000 to $30,000. Simply copy the model the banks use to help bring down your risk a little and maximize your return.

The simplest idea for being a lender is to offer private loans and charge interest. People often do this for family and friends. These loans require you to have some risk tolerance and backup funds. You must also be sure there is always a written legal contract so you have recourse should the person stop paying.

There is risk in acting like a lending bank yourself, but returns can be strong. Of course, you won't have insurance and government backing for the loans you issue. Nor might you have experience in checking the background, credit, employment, and stability of borrowers. So, get professional and legal advice before starting a venture like this. On my website at davidrhodd.com/privatelending, you'll find a quick introduction to private lending along with some FAQs. And my door is always open.

Leverage can be a lender's ally, but beware of going too far. Emulating a bank by being a lender has some risk, although success can bring substantial returns. Discussing it with financial professionals in this field, especially those who have worked with private lenders before, is essential. As I said, my door is always open. Call me any time or visit my website and schedule an appointment.

Secured Investment Checklist

When you're considering a secure investment, here is a handy checklist to review before you commit.

The Investment

1. How high is the return on this investment? Risk and return are proportional: the higher the return, the higher the risk.
2. Where does the interest I'll get paid come from? My own funds (interest reserve)? Cash flow of the investment? Or the interest paid by the borrower?

3. Where does my interest come from? Is my interest paid by the same company that I provided my cheque to?
4. What's the process of investing my money? Who touches my money? Which accounts does it go into? And does the name on the accounts match the company name?
5. What is the investment secured against?
6. What are my funds secured against? A promise? Collateral? Real estate? A trust account? Mortgage? A first-born child?
7. Is this a one-time investment or a long-term play?
8. Is it clear or confusing? Does it make sense or is it understandable only by the experts?
9. What are the unknowns related to this investment?

The Company

1. Who owns the company? Who are the principals and what is their background?
2. Is it a family-run business, arms-length entity, or are other people involved?
3. Is the company registered with any governing body?
4. What's the company's track record? Does it provide verifiable testimonials?
5. Does a Google search for scams involving the company or any of the people produce results?
6. Where is the company located? Locally or offshore?
7. How easily can they move locations?
8. How rooted is the company in the community? Is it in a temporary office? How long has it been there? Do I know anyone else who knows the company and who might have done business with it?
9. What is the company's street reputation? Is there any drama

or rumours when you mention the company name or its owners?

10. How accessible is it? Can I call the company and reach a human being? Does it respond to email?

11. What's in it for them? How does it make a profit on my investment? Why does it need my money?

12. How does the company respond to questions of potential conflict? When I ask about the risk of losing my money, or them running off with it, how do the company representatives react? What is their body language? What do they say?

13. Are they transparent? Are they protective of what they are doing, or is it an open book?

You

1. How do I feel at this moment? This is gut-check time. Am I comfortable? Scared? Nervous? Confident?

Create Safe Residual Income

To sum up, when you use your mortgage equity, I advise you to look for more secure investments and stay away from mutual funds and the stock market. This approach can lead you closer to your goal, which is to have continuous residual income that is secure and provides the lifestyle you want, without you having to trade your time and energy to create that revenue. Better to have investments that make money for you while you sleep as well as while you're awake. You're looking for secured investments that put your money to work for you – not the other way around – in a repeatable, residual way.

Your initial secured investments may begin by paying you as little as $500 each month. Good. Keep going. Continue applying the kinds of principles outlined in this book and, before you know it, you could be receiving $5,000 per month, then $10,000 or more.

Then the question is at what point between the $500 and $10,000 residual monthly income would you feel comfortable stepping away from your nine-to-five job? That threshold is different for each one of us, but know that it is attainable. I repeat: it is within your reach.

When you become a full-time investor, you will be taxed differently. The laws regarding taxation of income from investments are different from the tax laws for employment. With the right advice, you can benefit further from the investment life by reducing your taxes while still creating cash flow and acquiring assets. As you acquire properties, for example, banks are often willing to lend you more money against them. Imagine you own four properties. If you rent all of them out, paying the rental income into your mortgages increases your equity in those properties. That means the mortgages are being paid down while the properties are appreciating in value. Even after only three years, this has the possibility to create an additional $50,000 value for each of the four properties. Then you could apply that potential $50,000 x 4 = $200,000 to a new investment, or a child's tuition, or a dream vacation, or create a retirement account and have it pay you as a pension. These investments have now opened the door for you to change your lifestyle.

Enjoy the end goal of being financially free, free from an unfulfilling day job, if that's your dream, that hinders you from living the life you really desire. Get excited looking for that next secure investment. Follow sound advice. Weigh the risk of making the investment against the risk of letting your money sit in a bank or mutual fund. Then reap the rewards of the returns on your investments.

Remember to diversify your investments, too. Because no investment is guaranteed, it makes sense to make sure you have a pool of investments. That way if one runs into trouble, you have plenty of others to balance you out. Your mindset will help you weather the occasional investment blip – learn to expect some losses and take them in stride. As long as you have a good balance and variety in your investment portfolio, a loss here or there isn't going to sink you. It's part of the landscape.

Knowledge is indeed power. If you know better, you can do better.

* * *

9

CASH IN WITH A COACH

W hen you want to navigate to a specific destination, you have options for how to approach the task. You can use a GPS, or look at a map, or ask directions, or maybe follow a different method. Of all the options at your disposal, the most time-honoured is to follow the instructions of a trusted person who knows the way and has taken a precise route to that destination multiple times before.

That person may provide you with several details, like offering tips for easier travel and pointing out landmarks along the route to reduce confusion, to give a clearer understanding of how to reach the destination, to reduce distractions along the way, and to help you get there as efficiently as possible. Instead of wasting your time trying to figure out a travel route from scratch for yourself, then wasting more by encountering hurdles and delays and detours, it makes more sense to benefit from someone else's knowledge and experience so you can avoid difficulty in the first place.

Think of investing in a similar way. If you don't know how to invest in real estate, ask someone who has had repeated success with it. Surround yourself with experienced people who also align with your goals in life. I am here to help you, through this book, but I urge you to find a mentor, perhaps more than one, and get a coach.

Ask experienced people to show to you how to invest. Learn from them and follow their example. But be proactive. Take action to find these people. They will not come to you or fall into your lap.

I also provide this type of coaching service and you can get in touch by visiting davidrhodd.com.

Lessons in Learning and Life

Some years ago, in summer, my wife and I wanted to lay some patio stones in our backyard. After some thought, light research, and a few quotes from landscapers, we decided to do it all ourselves. How difficult could it be? It was just laying patio stones and we were smart, capable people. We were wrong. It was an excruciating and draining task for us. Not only did the job take much longer than it would have if we had hired professional contractors, we were exhausted, we were in pain, and the result was not even close to how we anticipated it would look. I completely underestimated the weight and pressure involved in lifting, arranging, placing, and securing each and every stone. Furthermore, I underestimated the level of skill required for the job.

As I reviewed what I had put my body through, and the results in my backyard, I concluded that I would have gladly paid the necessary costs to have that landscaping work completed by experts. The result would have been far better and I would have saved myself pain and stress. This experience reinforced what I already knew: that professionals in a particular field know much more than the average person who is viewing things from the outside. There is great value in the knowledge and experience of experts. Take their advice, follow their lead, and you will be pleased in the end.

Life lesson learned.

Being open to receive coaching is no different. Coaching is education, instruction, and training. It brings advice, information, and tips for a specific topic or area of expertise. In short, coaching brings knowledge, and knowledge is power. Sometimes you must pay for coaching, but a quality coach is worth it. A good coach is someone who has already achieved the very result you want for yourself. When a coach shares with you the experience and mistakes he/she has made on the road to success, it is hard to put a price on such knowledge.

We learn nothing from our successes. We learn from mistakes, even the mistakes of other people.

Consider an example using real estate. If you were to invest in real estate and make a small mistake, it might cost you anywhere from a few hundred to a few thousand dollars. If a few hundred dollars' worth of coaching can help you avoid losing a few thousand dollars, it is worth it.

If spending $5,000 on high level coaching could not only help you avoid losses, but also help you acquire an investment that appreciates by $50,000, that is very much worth the money. It stands to reason that gathering as many nuggets, gems, and clues as you can could make your real estate investment process more profitable and easier to navigate.

Sanjay

Sanjay is one of my most aggressive investment clients. When he first attended one of my investment seminars he was a director with one of the large utility companies, but he had been looking for a way to get into real estate. He was tired of working nine to five and felt there was more he could do with his life.

Then he was surprised with a termination package in one of the many rounds of corporate downsizing so common in the post-2008 economy. He called it a blessing in disguise. He was going to use some of the proceeds from his package to start investing in real estate. He asked me to coach him and teach him everything I knew. His objective was to earn $2,000 each month.

We started in rent-to-own. I coached Sanjay through his first deal. Then his second. Sanjay trusted me because I'd done it, and he put any fear he may have felt aside and kept thinking about his objective. Today Sanjay has seven properties in total and his income is triple what he initially aimed for.

A Coach for Investing and Life

There is a proviso, of course. Engaging a coach does not guarantee that you won't have failures or make mistakes. But it can help you avoid common mistakes and provide you with deeper insight. Exploring the world of real estate investment without guidance is never advisable and is often a recipe for disaster. Coaching can turn the odds more in your favour and show you the mistakes to avoid.

My advice that you should find investment coaches and mentors is about more than merely making money or becoming wealthy. You have many gifts inside you that you must share with others. You are unique in this world and the rest of us will be disadvantaged if we are unable to see and appreciate those gifts of yours. You owe it to yourself, to your next generation, and to the world to do this.

Imagine you achieve the goals you have set for yourself and become the person you truly want to be. Imagine living a life of abundance where your dreams are fulfilled. Imagine then sharing your gifts with the world. How many people would you affect? How many would you help? How many lives could be changed for the better if you are achieving your true purpose on this earth?

This is why it is mandatory that you change your mindset and take action *now*. This is not only about you. It is about the generations following that are depending on you. Find your investment mentors now. Take these actions today so that others may benefit tomorrow. When you think this way, you are less likely to become complacent. Much is depending on you.

Earlier in my career, many wonderful individuals imparted advice and guidance to me. One of the greatest mistakes I made was not recognizing the value of what these coaches and mentors told me. For years, I maintained the mentality of, 'Why would I pay somebody money to coach me when I can learn it all on my own?'. The time it might take me to learn never intimidated me. Nor was I ever fearful to take action, so I thought learning, growing, falling, and failing were all part of the process. (Which they are!) To my surprise, as I grew older and more mature, I began to realize that knowledge truly is power and that I could receive that power from others instead of doing everything the hard way. I finally recognized that coaching is essentially a shortcut to creating success. As I listened to coaches and gathered more information, my thinking changed and I asked myself, "Why would I *not* take advantage of the life lessons, experience, and advice of those in the same industry who have gone before me?"

Please learn from my mistakes.

Accountability

A great benefit of coaching is how it can hold you accountable to yourself as well as to your coach. People who have someone guiding them, someone to report to, and someone who is checking in often achieve more than those who learn exclusively on their own. The idea of having someone watching and helping can be motivating and even apply a certain pressure to succeed.

If you pay for coaching, you want to get your money's worth. That is motivating as well.

As mentioned earlier, when you know your purpose, have a clear mindset, acquire all the necessary knowledge and mechanics, and know who you are going to bless, you ultimately have your blueprint for success. Instead of confusion, you will have an easy-to-understand, step-by-step guide to achieving your desired result.

But you still need accountability. Being accountable to somebody can help you remain true to your purpose and goals. It may also help you stop taking the very tempting easy way out where near enough is good enough.

Think of accountability like having a personal trainer at the gym. If you set a goal to perform 20 push-ups, your trainer will praise you for that and then push you to do more. In contrast, if you train by yourself, you may be tempted to say that 20 push-ups are enough, pat yourself on the back for the achievement, and stop without exploring your true potential. A trainer or coach will hold you accountable and you will hold yourself accountable in return. When encouraged to do five or 10 more push-ups, you will respond by doing your level best to achieve the goal and go beyond what you thought were your limits. "You can do it! You can do it!" Amazingly, your mind and body will give it everything.

Having somebody else to hold you accountable can make results much better and more satisfying.

Choose Your Coach

When I set myself a goal, I identify clearly and specifically where I want to be. Then I look for people who are already there and find out how I can get closer to them. This is what Sanjay did. He knew what he was interested in. He found my seminar, signed up, and then followed through and asked me to coach him into becoming the investor he wanted to be.

In-person, direct coaching is always best. But inevitably some are not accessible in person. At this point, I refer to anything I can get my hands on: books, articles, videos, podcasts, and so on. It is not the same as in-person coaching, but the authors are still mentoring and influencing me.

As I was growing up, I was amazed that I could find correlations between my situation and that of a financial giant like Michael Lee-Chin. This really opened my mind. Michael is a billionaire Canadian and Jamaican investor and philanthropist who literally was a self-starter on the journey to financial success. I could identify with him and look to him as a role model. Although our journeys began at different times, we both initially entered engineering. Michael focused on being a civil engineer, while I headed towards mechanical. We both eventually took a leap from traditional engineering to financial services, where we each ran independent companies. I was not aware at first how my engineering background would become an asset in the financial world, but today I bring my engineering thinking to create financial solutions for my clients, using their biggest assets to create greater wealth for future generations.

No matter how successful you already are, you should always have a mentor and/or role model whose journey gives you hope, inspiration, and the ability to dream. That is how Michael Lee-Chin is (indirectly) helping me on my life's journey. At the time of writing this book, Michael is estimated to be worth more than $2 billion (Canadian). Yet he came from a beginning similar to mine. That demonstrates to me that I have no excuses because he achieved his success with similar skill sets to mine and the same opportunities as I have.

Since being inspired by Michael Lee-Chin and entering financial services, I surrounded myself with some of the best coaches in the world. Robert G. Allen, J.T. Fox, and Brian Tracy have all coached me. I thank them profusely for their guidance.

Choose your financial coach to be your role model and to share in your purpose. Surrounding yourself with the very best successful people will increase your chances of succeeding. Choose a coach that has experience in the areas you are interested in learning more about, too. I offer coaching services, and my financial services expertise is as follows:

- Free government down-payment assistance programs.
- Rent-to-own housing program.
- Mortgage pre-approvals.
- Refinancing.
- Fixed-rate mortgages.
- Variable-rate mortgages.
- Second mortgages.
- Private financing.
- Debt consolidation.
- Home equity loans and renovation financing.
- Downsizing and upgrading financing.
- Reverse mortgages.
- Mortgage insurance.
- Mortgages for rental properties.
- Mortgage renewals.
- New-to-Canada mortgages.
- Credit repair assistance.

- Self-employed mortgages.
- Vacation home financing.
- Learn how to pay off your mortgage faster.
- Learn more about investment properties.
- Reduce your taxes payable.
- Learn how to make 8-15 per cent returns in your RRSPs and investments.
- How to invest in headache-free real estate and make 20 per cent returns.
- And more!

If any of these areas are of interest to you, I'd be happy to help. Reach out to me at davidrhodd.com to schedule an appointment today.

* * *

10

ABUNDANCE AND GRATITUDE

B lessing others is my personal credo for life. I have no doubt that it is through giving that we truly receive. I believe that those of us who have been fortunate enough to experience success are more or less obligated to give others the benefit of our experience and encourage them to find their own success.

Even if you don't share my beliefs, I hope that this book and your new journey toward financial freedom will assist you in finding your life's truth and mission. It is vital for you to learn exactly what makes you a complete, happy person and then apply that approach to your life, including to your business and financial dealings. Doing this will solidify your purpose. When you start giving back, you will find that it is not only self-fulfilling, it acts as your contribution to the betterment of society.

This is an important step on the pathway to abundance.

Scarcity Vs Abundance

Scarcity is the opposite of abundance. We live in a world dominated by an attitude of scarcity. Just look at all the marketing and advertising that is designed to make us think we are lacking something so we will go out and buy what they offer.

I used to work from the scarcity mindset. When I sat down with prospective clients I would be worried about how much to tell them, afraid that they'd receive the knowledge I gave them and then take their business somewhere else. I'd think about the time I was investing (an hour, maybe two at the most) and I'd fret about not getting a return on that hour. I've learned the value and importance of switching to an abundance mindset.

Today I sit with clients and prospective clients and my sole purpose is to pour as much value into that meeting and their life as possible. When I operate from a position of abundance and I work to spread as much goodness as I can, I know what comes around goes around. My needs will be taken care of when I first take care of the needs of others. So, I give everyone – prospects, clients, attendees at my seminars, patrons at the trade shows I participate in – all the value I have as if they were sent here to to see me; as if I'm the only person who can give them this information and they only have this moment in time. The payoff for me is that maybe, just maybe, there's a chance it will change their lives for the better.

Abundance is about seeing what you have and appreciating it. Understanding and creating abundance requires a deliberate effort to see the gifts you already have for what they are. Those gifts start with you and your purpose in life. You have been given so much already in your life. See those things. See the people around you and the gifts they bring to you.

You are fortunate enough to have been born at a time when there are more blessings, advantages, and opportunities in society than at any other time in human history.

Recognizing and appreciating abundance becomes a self-fulfilling prophecy. It creates a cycle of abundance, where you and others give what you receive and receive what you give.

I firmly believe that when you become wealthy and financially free, that position is not intended merely to bless you, but to become a blessing for those around you and the many you will encounter along your journey. When you create wealth for yourself, it isn't just an avenue for selfishness. Enjoy some of the comforts and new possibilities wealth brings to your life, but you will appreciate true satisfaction only when you start to affect other's lives in a positive fashion.

If you look at some of the wealthiest people, you will notice many are very generous with their money and their energies. They give significant portions of their fortunes to friends, family, charities, foundations, causes, research, and many other avenues. Consider Bill Gates, for example. At one time, he was the richest person in the world. He and his wife have given away $28 billion to help others. Gates has realized who he truly is and he works to this day to help the poorest and sickest people around the globe.

Giving is a pure act from the heart, with no expectation of anything in return. Because of its purity, selfless giving will start a cycle of goodness around you. The more you give, the more you receive. The premise seems a little ironic when you consider that, after working so hard to finally reach the position where money is not a concern and you can afford your ultimate lifestyle, giving money to others may start more money and wealth flowing your way. The principle is very similar to karma. You reap what you sow.

Of course, giving freely and copiously is not the same as blowing or wasting your money. You should give using the exact same life purpose you used to attain your wealth and create abundance. Share your true gifts in whatever capacity you can. Provide others with encouragement and support in your unique way so that they may have opportunities to grow and appreciate abundance themselves.

Giving is the way to happiness, just as being greedy and selfish is the way to misery. I think it is much harder to achieve the goal of financial freedom with a mindset focused only on hoarding wealth and over-indulging in it. I believe that, to become wealthy or financially free, each of us needs to have a greater destiny, a greater purpose, and a greater calling in our lives. Hence my personal philosophy is to give back as much as I can, so that I may bless other people.

Some might say giving is a sacrament, an outward and visible sign of an inward and spiritual grace. It is certainly an outward expression of something that truly makes our souls feel good. Among our simplest needs as human beings are the need to belong to a group and the need to be loved. Giving to others is the best way to fulfill those needs.

Create the Life You Want

Having a great deal of money at your disposal can be positive. Equally, it can be negative. Much depends on how you use your money. Therefore, know your purpose in life and what makes you truly happy. Keep those in mind as you go through your blueprint for building your financially free life. Have a clear end goal, work hard and smart to get there, but never lose sight of where you came from and what influence you can have to advance the people and world around you.

Who will you bless when you get to your goal? Who will you help along the journey? How will you show gratitude? The answers to these questions will be crucial in creating your life of abundance.

When you are financially free and not dependent on cash, to whom will you give the benefits of your learning? When you have no need to worry about bills or a mortgage or a food budget, who will you help? When you can go on that vacation you have always wanted and do the things your heart truly desires, who will you encourage to achieve the same? When you are fulfilling your needs and receiving blessings, how will you change someone's life for the better? Picture yourself helping others, teaching them new things, bringing value and growth to their lives. Learn to give now. Then give again. And again. Continue the cycle of giving and being grateful, then watch the blessings overflow.

The journey to financial freedom may seem huge for you right now. You may even feel overwhelmed by the challenge and not know where to start. Maybe you are unsure where your next dollar will come from. You start by taking one footstep. Then a second. Then a third. The journey of 1,000 miles begins with a single step. That first step is the decision to embark on the journey and it is the hardest step of all. The second is to uncover what makes you truly happy. (Hint: it is already within you.) The third step is to put that approach to happiness into everything you do. *Everything*. Live it. Don't let it be just a belief. Make it an active commitment every day. Take these three steps with truth and love and your next dollar will be there. Be grateful for it and continue your journey. Keep following your roadmap to success, wealth, and abundance. When you know your purpose and destination, you will be able to recognize that the hurdles you encounter along the journey are not actually roadblocks but challenges from which you can learn. Maybe you will stumble on these loose stones. But be assured they will not stop you completing your journey. You *will* find your footing again.

When challenges present themselves, welcome them. Be grateful for the messages they send. Work through them using your purpose and philosophy for life to guide you. Acquiring wealth does not mean you avoid all adversity. All things that are worth doing, having, and risking will bring challenges. How you respond to adversity will determine your success at overcoming it. The fact that you are embarking on this new life of financial freedom is proof that you are willing to handle adversity in a positive way.

Maybe your pathway to success will not be entirely straight. No one said it had to be straight. But don't change your roadmap. It works. Keep following it step by step. You will learn, grow, and experience some of life's most valuable lessons along the journey. Stay focused, disciplined, and determined to get where you need to be and live the life of your dreams.

Stay true to yourself and you will get there.

> *"Often people attempt to live their lives backwards: they try to have more things, or more money, in order to do more of what they want so that they will be happier.*
>
> *The way it actually works is the reverse. You must first be who you really are, then do what you need to do in order to have what you want."*
>
> — MARGARET YOUNG, AMERICAN SINGER AND ACTRESS

11

REVIEW THE STEPS

I have shared a lot of information for you in the preceding chapters. To help tie it all together and reinforce what you've read, I've distilled the information into the most important steps. Along your journey, you can check in with this chapter and be reminded of what's next and what to prepare for. You'll know which chapter to go back to if you need to refresh your memory in more detail. Follow these steps and soon you will be ready to enter the ranks of the financially independent.

Step 1: Adopt the Mindset of Millionaires

Go after what you want. Keep the big picture in mind while you take care of the small details.

Embrace the value of, and lessons in, mistakes. Wealthy people gather the learnings from these mistakes and challenging experiences and move on. Understand that adversity plays an important role in life: it teaches, it builds, it reveals.

Stay above the negativity you may encounter around you. Don't let the misery of others get in your way.

Practice saying, "I can. I am worthy." And think positively about money. This is when doors will start to open for you and the road starts to take you to financial independence.

Step 2: Find Your Purpose

Some people are called to their purpose. Others accidentally uncover their purpose. Still others work hard to reveal it. There is no single best way, or best formula, for finding your purpose. The key factors are:

1. the awareness that your purpose lies within you, not outside you, and
2. the commitment to find it, nurture it, and take action on it.

You know what it is: something you are passionate about, that motivates you. Follow the eight steps to identifying your purpose:

1. Start a journal.
2. Get to know yourself. Explore your core values, your moral code. What pushes your buttons? What brings you joy?
3. What is at the top of your interest list? What are you doing when time flies?
4. Create an inventory of all your talents and skills. Reach back to childhood and add well-loved but forgotten hobbies to the list.
5. How do you want to impact the world? Why do you want to impact the world in this way?
6. What does the world need? Your purpose and how you want

to impact the world must align with an actual need in the world.

7. Keep company with people you find inspiring, those already doing what you want to do.
8. Face the fear of change and refuse to let it hold you back.

Whatever your purpose, discovering and working toward achieving it will get you out of the default life. No more mindless cycle of wake, work, eat, watch, sleep, repeat. No more doldrums of feeling stuck in a job you hate. Make it the temporary vehicle that will help you achieve your purpose.

Step 3: Nurture Your Credit Score

If you don't know what your credit score is, find out. Ensure there are no errors on your credit file. If there are errors, correct them. Take the necessary steps to get your credit score as far above 650 as you can – and keep it there. Above 700 is better. Understand the factors that affect your credit score and make adjustments in your life as necessary. Use credit, but use it wisely. Pay all your bills on time. Don't close out old credit accounts unless absolutely necessary.

Step 4: Take Care of Cash Flow, Debt, Taxes

Track all of your spending for 30 days. Adjust your spending behaviour as necessary. Establish and stick to a cash flow plan that includes eliminating your debt. Reduce your tax payable. Taxes are a major expense for us all. Paying them will be a reality as long as you are working a job, and that is why it is essential to find the means to constantly reduce your taxable income.

The involvement in self-employed operations or owning businesses allow you to control your tax payable at least to some degree.

Owning a business is one of the best ways to reduce taxes. Being an investor is considered the same as being a business owner, as you're considered to be managing multiple properties.

If you have to get creative and turn your hobby into a business, do that. Whether it is teaching people guitar lessons, or fixing cars, make it an official business. I offer a course that can teach you how to do this successfully. Check it out at davidrhodd.com. Owning a business allows you to write off some expenses. The total amount of expenses per year are deducted from your total earnings, which leads you to be taxed on the lowest possible income.

For example, you made $40,000 for the year, but had $10,000 worth of expenses. The $10,000 is deducted from the $40,000 of income, leaving you with a total income of $30,000, dropping you to a lower tax rate. A certified accountant will always be able to assist you further with more information on how to make this work. But the concept on opening your own small business to reduce your taxes is not a far stretch for many.

Step 5: Learn from the Banks

Take back control and put your money to work for you. Build up to a place where you put money to work for you: leverage borrowed money to buy other assets that will increase in value and produce a revenue stream. Pay down your mortgage so that you have room to use the equity to expand your real estate portfolio. Want help paying down your mortgage? Do what thousands before you have done: follow the system at davidpayoffmymortgage.com.

Step 6: Stop Renting – Be a Home Owner

As a renter, you don't have the opportunity to create equity through the simple act of paying your rent. As a home owner, your rent is your monthly mortgage payment. Start with owning your principal residence, and soon you will create the opportunity to leverage that equity into owning more properties and generating passive income. Explore all options available to you to help you get into a home. Save for your down payment or borrow some from family or friends. Check out my rent-to-own program. But buy a home and then start paying down your mortgage.

Step 7: Leverage Your Equity

Resist the temptation to leave the equity sitting there. Look at the big picture and leverage that equity to your advantage. As you pay down your mortgage, you create room in your mortgage and your home increases in value. Put that unused equity to work. Find safe, secure and predictable real estate investments that will provide you with profitable returns.

Step 8: Choose Secured Investments

My bias, as you know by now, is toward real estate investments. They are secured investments and make more sense to me than investing in the stock market or mutual funds. A piece of property is real, tangible, and you can visit it and see that it is still there. It has real value and security and you can easily sell the property to someone else or rent it out to recoup your money or generate revenue.

What qualifies as a secure investment is something that has at least the equivalent value or more.

Investing in real estate properties, mortgages, and tax liens are three asset-backed investments that are secure. Once you have found the right secure investment, ensure an interest rate of as close to double your mortgage interest rate to make a positive return on your investment. The key is to double up on your investments and be aware of the *rule of 72.*

Soon you can leave that day job you hate so much and reap the benefits of the monthly cash flow you are receiving from all the investments. Once you are making anywhere between $5,000 to $10,000 a month in passive income you can assess if that can replace your employment income for a comfortable life. If this scares you, explore the option of waiting until the money has doubled.

Move into the driver's seat and control your destiny. Make more profitable, predictable returns for your retirement.

Don't feel bad about borrowing to invest. You know if you are borrowing at two or three per cent and getting a return rate of eight or 15 per cent, it is all worth it.

Debt is not the final number. How much your debt is making is more important. This is the blueprint. Keep doing this and you will soon be walking in financial freedom. The mortgages will start to reduce, and everything will start to fall into place.

How I Work

There are two common question I get asked: "How do I work with you?" and "How do you get paid?"

I get paid from services that I perform. If you were to come to me for business and financial coaching, I usually work on a monthly retainer. If you were to take one of my coaching courses, you would pay for the course. If you wanted to continue with coaching after the course, you'd pay a monthly retainer.

If I arrange a mortgage for you, I usually get paid by the mortgage company. Sometimes a mortgage is complex and needs more work, in which case I get paid out of the mortgage proceeds. In either case, there is nothing for you to pay out of pocket.

For investment services, my commission is factored into the investments themselves. I work on the principle that an investor will never pay me out of their pocket unless they're making money. This creates a win-win situation, which is always my goal.

100 Success Stories

I'm already working on my next book: *100 Success Stories*. I am hand-selecting a core group of 100 people, past clients, referrals, and prospects. I will help them create the means to achieve their financial dreams, and then I will tell the story of our journey together.

Want to apply?

If you're reading this book and you want to see if any of the 100 spots are still open, reach out to me at davidrhodd.com.

My Power Team

I've made several references throughout this book to the importance of having a good team around you to support your progress toward financial freedom. If you don't have these key roles in place, you can see my power team list at davidrhodd.com/powerteam.

* * *

ABOUT THE AUTHOR

David Rhodd is a Toronto-based mortgage broker, entrepreneur, trainer, and wealth creator inspired to write *House Rich Cash Poor? No More!* because of his profound belief in the power and possibility of becoming financially independent. David has studied the science of money achievement and motivation and mastered it in practice by interviewing hundreds of successful business leaders, collaborating with them in the boardroom, and translating theory into bottom line results for his clients. A dynamic personality and sought after motivational speaker, David has helped thousands of people in business and professional circles, from Fortune 500 CEOs and small business owners to non-profit and community leaders.

David's focus is on home buyers and owners who want help dealing with mortgages and financial issues. He offers his clients expertise in mortgage issues and leveraging home equity to build wealth. He has assisted and coached many to realize above average returns on their investment portfolios and liquid cash using his knowledge of alternative investments such as foreign exchange, commodities, real estate, and mortgage investing.

Get Inspired. Be Influential. Bless others. These are the tenets on which David bases his entire business approach.

SUGGESTED READING

Cashflow Quadrant: Rich Dad's Guide to Financial Freedom

— ROBERT T. KIYOSAKI

Change Your Thinking, Change Your Life

— BRIAN TRACY

Is Your Mortgage Tax Deductible? The Smith Manoeuvre

— FRASER SMITH

Nothing Down for the 2000s: Dynamic New Wealth Strategies in Real Estate

— ROBERT ALLEN

Nothing Down: How to Buy Real Estate With Little or No Money Down

— ROBERT ALLEN

Rich Dad, Poor Dad: What the Rich Teach Their Kids About Money That the Poor and Middle Class Do Not!

— ROBERT KIYOSAKI

The Power of Self Confidence

— BRIAN TRACY

* * *

REFERENCES

(n.d.). Retrieved from Deposits.org: https://canada.deposits.org/

(n.d.). Retrieved from Deposits.org: http://us.deposits.org

Allen, R. G. (1984). *Nothing Down: How to Buy Real Estate With Little or No Money Down*. New York: Simon & Schuster.

Allen, R. G. (2004). *Nothing Down for the 2000s: Dynamic New Wealth Strategies in Real Estate*. New York: Free Press.

Bondarenko, P. (n.d.). *5 of the World's Most-Devastating Financial Crises*. Retrieved from Encyclopaedia Britannica: https://www.britannica.com/list/5-of-the-worlds-most-devastating-financial-crises

Canada Deposit Insurance Corporation. (2017). *History of member institution failures*. Retrieved from Canada Deposit Insurance Corporation: http://www.cdic.ca/en/about-cdic/resolution/Pages/history.aspx

Canadian Bankers Association. (2016, October 4). *Issue Brief: Global*

Banking Regulations and Banks in Canada. Retrieved from Canadian Bankers Association: http://www.cba.ca/global-banking-regulations-and-banks-in-canada

Canadian Business. (2015, December 24). *Canada's Richest People: Michael Lee-Chin.* Retrieved from Canadian Business: http://www.canadianbusiness.com/lists-and-rankings/richest-people/rich-100-michael-lee-chin/

Carlyle, E. (2016, March 14). *The 20 Richest Real Estate Barons In The World 2016.* Retrieved from Forbes: http://www.forbes.com/sites/erincarlyle/2016/03/14/the-20-richest-real-estate-barons-in-the-world-2016/#54e2146e34cf

Cawley, C. (2016, April 18). *The '8 out of 10 Startups Fail' Statistic Is a Myth.* Retrieved from TechCo: https://tech.co/startup-failure-statistic-myth-2016-04

CBC News. (2008, October 15). *The end is here for 40-year mortgages.* Retrieved from CBC News Business: http://www.cbc.ca/news/business/the-end-is-here-for-40-year-mortgages-1.745656

Delmendo, L. C. (2017, April 2). *The amazing Canadian boom - house prices are surging!* Retrieved from Global Property Guide: http://www.globalpropertyguide.com/North-America/Canada/Price-History

Elliott, R. (2008, December 11). *In Crisis, Canadian Banks Survive And Thrive.* Retrieved from Forbes: https://www.forbes.com/2008/12/11/canada-banking-crisis-oped-cx_re_1211elliott.html#2526758c2e50

Flipping For Profit. (n.d.). *Hard Money Lenders in Canada.* Retrieved from Flipping For Profit Canadian:

http://www.flipping4profit.ca/private-hard-money-lenders-in-canada/hard-money-lenders-in-canada/

Forbes. (2018). *The World's Billionaires.* Retrieved from Forbes: http://www.forbes.com/billionaires/list/

Freed, D. (2014, October 13). *How the 10 Biggest Banks Make Money Now Might Surprise You.* Retrieved from The Street: https://www.thestreet.com/story/12909997/11/how-the-10-biggest-banks-make-money-now-might-surprise-you.html

Hough, J. (2014, August 12). *Canadians pay 42% of income in tax — more than they spend on food, shelter, clothing combined.* Retrieved from National Post: http://nationalpost.com/news/canada/canadians-pay-42-of-income-in-tax-more-than-they-spend-on-food-shelter-clothing-combined

HSBC. (2016). *The Future of Retirement: Generations and Journeys.* HSBC.

Hyman, S., Pennycook, C., Vesey, D., & Williams, N. (2015). Canada. In J. Putnis (Ed.), *The Banking Regulation Review* (6 ed., pp. 114-128). Gideon Roberton. Retrieved from https://www.dwpv.com/~/media/Files/PDF_EN/2015/2015-06-26-The-Banking-Regulation-Review-Canada.ashx

Investopedia. (2017). *Assignment.* Retrieved from Investopedia: http://www.investopedia.com/terms/a/assignment.asp

Investopedia. (2017). *Equity.* Retrieved from Investopedia: http://www.investopedia.com/terms/e/equity.asp

Investopedia. (2017). *FDIC Insured Account.* Retrieved from Investopedia: https://www.investopedia.com/terms/f/fdic-insured-account.asp

Investopedia. (2017, November 20). *Understanding the Mortgage*

Payment Structure. Retrieved from Investopedia: http://www.investopedia.com/articles/pf/05/022405.asp

Isidore, C. (2016, April 28). *35 bankers were sent to prison for financial crisis crimes*. Retrieved from CNN Money: http://money.cnn.com/2016/04/28/news/companies/bankers-prison/

Karl, W. (2016, February 22). *A Look At Canada's Housing Performance Over Time*. Retrieved from Huffington Post (Canada): http://www.huffingtonpost.ca/ypnexthome/canadas-housing-performance_b_9266608.html

King, R. (2015, August 19). *6 mistakes new condo investors make*. Retrieved from MoneySense: http://www.moneysense.ca/spend/real-estate/income-properties/5-mistakes-new-condo-investors-make/

Kiyosaki, R. T., & Lechter, S. L. (1997). *Rich Dad, Poor Dad*. New York: Warner Books, Inc.

Kiyosaki, R. T., & Lechter, S. L. (1998, revised 2011). *Cashflow Quadrant: Rich Dad's Guide to Financial Freedom*. Paradise Valley, AZ: TechPress.

Long, H. (2016, January 2014). *ATM and overdraft fees top $6 billion at the big 3 banks*. Retrieved from CNN Money: http://money.cnn.com/2016/01/14/investing/atm-overdraft-fees/

Marr, G. (2016, May 24). *Four out of 10 homeowners caught short without enough money to meet their expenses*. Retrieved from Financial Post: http://business.financialpost.com/personal-finance/debt/four-out-of-10-homeowners-caught-short-without-enough-money-to-meet-their-expenses-new-survey-finds

Palacios, M., Lammam, C., & Ren, F. (2016, August). *Taxes versus the Necessities of Life: The Canadian Consumer Tax Index, 2016 edition.*

Retrieved from Fraser Institute: https://www.fraserinstitute.org/sites/default/files/canadian-consumer-tax-index-2016.pdf

Passino, C. (2016, May 19). *Slow And Steady: Real Estate Growth In World Cities Is An Exercise In Moderation.* Retrieved from Forbes: http://www.forbes.com/sites/carlapassino/2016/05/19/slow-and-steady-real-estate-growth-in-world-cities-is-an-exercise-in-moderation/#68df4fe049c6

Perry, B. (n.d.). *Safety and Income: Real Assets - Gold, Real Estate and Collectibles.* Retrieved from Investopedia: http://www.investopedia.com/university/safety-and-income/real-assets.asp

Porter, T. (2010). Canadian banks in the financial and economic crisis. *Policy Responses to Unfettered Finance Workshop.* Ottawa: North-South Institute.

Pryor, K. (2016, January 12). *Here Are the Startup Failure Rates by Industry.* Retrieved from TechCo: http://tech.co/startup-failure-rates-industry-2016-01

Schmidt, M. (2017). *Margins in Business, Finance, and Investing .* Retrieved from Solution Matrix Ltd.: https://www.business-case-analysis.com/margin.html

Schwab, K. (2010). *The Global Competitiveness Report 2010-2011.* Geneva: World Economic Forum. Retrieved from http://www3.weforum.org/docs/WEF_GlobalCompetitivenessReport_2010-11.pdf

Shillington, R. (2016, February). *An Analysis of the Economic Circumstances of Canadian Seniors.* Retrieved from Broadbent Institute: https://d3n8a8pro7vhmx.cloudfront.net/broadbent/pages/4904/att

achments/original/1455216659/An_Analysis_of_the_Economic_Circ umstances_of_Canadian_Seniors.pdf?1455216659

Smith, F. (2002). *The Smith Manoeuvre.* Outspan Publishing.

Smith, M. N. (2016, July 26). *The 16 industries most likely to make you a millionaire.* Retrieved from Business Insider UK: http://uk.businessinsider.com/industries-that-will-drive-millionaire-growth-according-to-the-world-wealth-report-2016-7/

Stammers, R. (2017, December 7). *Top 4 Things That Determine a Home's Value.* Retrieved from Investopedia: http://www.investopedia.com/articles/mortgages-real-estate/08/housing-appreciation.asp

Stein, G. (2016, February 25). *New insights on bank overdraft fees and 4 ways to avoid them.* Retrieved from Consumer Financial Protection Bureau: https://www.consumerfinance.gov/about-us/blog/new-insights-on-bank-overdraft-fees-and-4-ways-to-avoid-them/

Tweedie, N. (2013, January 18). *Bill Gates interview: I have no use for money. This is God's work.* Retrieved from The Telegraph: http://www.telegraph.co.uk/technology/bill-gates/9812672/Bill-Gates-interview-I-have-no-use-for-money.-This-is-Gods-work.html

Wikipedia. (2017). *List of largest U.S. bank failures.* Retrieved from Wikipedia: https://en.wikipedia.org/wiki/List_of_largest_U.S._bank_failures

Wikipedia. (n.d.). *Michael Lee-Chin.* Retrieved from Wikipedia: https://en.wikipedia.org/wiki/Michael_Lee-Chin

Workopolis. (2016, September 14). *What you need to earn to buy a house in every major Canadian city.* Retrieved from Workopolis: http://careers.workopolis.com/advice/how-much-you-need-to-earn-to-buy-a-house-in-every-major-canadian-city/

www.ingramcontent.com/pod-product-compliance
Lightning Source LLC
Chambersburg PA
CBHW060029210326
41520CB00009B/1052